*AN ADVENTURE IN LOVE*

CHRISTIAN FAMILY LIVING

*An Adventure in Love*

W. Taliaferro Thompson

John Knox Press

RICHMOND, VIRGINIA

Library of Congress Catalog Card Number: 56-6717

To my wife, through whom our children and I have been led into a better understanding of the love and integrity of God.

# Foreword

Another book on the home! Yet people stop reading older books, feeling that they are outmoded, and turn to those just published in the hope that they will find something new and final. But there is not much that is new, and so little that is final. The mood today is one of humility. One of the wisest writers in the field of child study confesses, "We know so little, yet, about human behaviour. We have to feel our way" It is in that spirit that this book is written, with the hope that someone will be helped a bit toward a better understanding of life in the home.

While I have read almost innumerable books, I have probably learned more in other ways. For over thirty years I have taught courses in Understanding Children, and in Understanding Youth, at Union Theological Seminary and at the General Assembly's Training School for Lay Workers in Richmond, Virginia. Hundreds of thoughtful men and women have taken questionnaires to parents and to boys and girls, and have given me of their wisdom in papers and classroom discussions.

For twenty-three summers I was Associate Director and Director of Religious Work at a camp enrolling from one hundred fifty to two hundred boys. During most of these summers I lived in a cabin with several boys and was associated with them day and night. They taught me some things I had not found in books—and vitally.

My real teacher has been our home, where I had the joy of watching six children grow into fine manhood and womanhood largely through the influence of their mother, who put into practice the principles I was discussing with my classes.

If I have learned anything at all from these varied experiences it is that as we think of creating a good home, the emphasis must be on life—the whole life—rather than on techniques. For the growth of parents and children alike is largely a matter of interpersonal relationships, which depend for their value on the Christian character of those involved.

T. H. L. Parker in his brief biography of the great Reformer says, "Calvin was born to write." That certainly is not true in my case. Writing is a labor, if not a torment. This book would not have been started but for the insistence of Rev. William P. Anderson, Jr., Director of Adult and Family Education of the Board of Christian Education of the Presbyterian Church in the U. S.; and it would never have been finished without the encouragement of my wife, and the clerical help of Mrs. W. T. Cosby. My gratitude is theirs.

W. TALIAFERRO THOMPSON.

# Contents

# Contents

*". . . So faith, hope, love abide . . .*
*but the greatest of these is love. Make love*
*your aim."*
I Corinthians 13:13—14:1. (R.S.V.)

# Yesterday and Today

*F*AMILY LIFE, TODAY, can be basically a deep and lasting friendship, the richest, most creative that life knows, in which individuals are kept together not by neighborhood pressure, nor their needs created by an older culture, but largely by their need for the Christian love that belongs to such a relationship. If we can only see this clearly, family life can be richer and more meaningful than ever before in our history.

## The Values of Yesterday

Family life involves personal relationships, but the family is also a social institution, profoundly affected by changes taking place in the social order. So an understanding of what present-day family life can be is achieved, in part, by reflecting upon what has happened to our culture during the last century, or century and a half. And even though a generalization cannot be wholly accurate, since it does not recognize differences between families in different sections of our country, nor differences between rural and urban family life, a generalization is necessary to sharpen the picture.

In other years a man married a girl from a nearby farm and established his home on a part of his father's land, or brought his wife to the rough house he had built in the clearing created by his own labor. Certain values which were very real inhered in the family brought into being in this way.

*Marriage was the one way both man and woman could achieve independence.* The man was a part of a patriarchal family, under the dominance of his father, and could not be his own master until he created a separate establishment. The woman often was not much more than a servant at the beck and call of her parents. No work in the community was available to her, and her one hope for a life of her own was through marriage. While she usually had to be subordinate to her husband, nevertheless in a sense the home was hers, and she was its mistress. In some parts of New England single persons of either sex were forbidden to live alone. As recently as a hundred years ago, no woman unaccompanied by a man could enter a restaurant or a hotel.

*Marriage offered the man decided economic values.* His wife belonged to him and all that she earned was his. If she was from a home of wealth she brought a dowry with her. From the beginning of their life together she was his business partner, without pay, working with him in the field and at the lighter tasks in the home and garden.

*Marriage usually resulted in children, who were a great asset.* The pioneer home could hardly get along without a half-dozen or more. Children were not so much mouths to feed as hands to work under the direction of an authoritarian father, who looked forward to their taking care of him when he was old. Adam Smith, comparing old Europe with young America, said that there a widow with four or five children had no chance to marry. In the new country she would be eagerly sought as one who possessed a fortune.[1]

The woman, as already made clear, did not fare so well. Nothing was hers. Her husband could even give away her children. She worked early and late, and often when quite young wore herself out through child-bearing and her multiplied labors. Few wives outlived their husbands. A study of pioneer graveyards shows the head of the household laid to rest surrounded by his wives—two, three, even four or five. But she had no other chance to support herself away from her father's house and was probably freer in a home that seemed to be her own. Should her husband die first, then the farm would be hers.

*The home gave its members a sense of security.* For the family of those years the home was a self-sufficient unit. Its members raised or made most of the things they ate or wore. With the shutters pulled tight, a log fire roaring in the wide fireplace, let the storm rage without! It was the man's castle and in it the woman felt protected and safe from the perils of the rough world outside.

*The home was a school and a church.* There were no schools near, so that learning was a part of children's life in the home, with their mother as the teacher. There were few churches, and only occasional services, so that the home became the center of worship with the father as the priest. Such religious instruction as was given was provided by the parents. Should they have opportunity to go to church, all sat side by side in the family pew.

*The home provided its own recreation.* It was in the home that friends were entertained in simple ways, and the family as a whole went to husking-bees, barn-raisings, square dances, or other such community recreation that brought people together. Because often long distances separated a family from its neighbors it had to depend largely upon its own members for fellowship.

The family was a close-knit group, together twenty-four hours a day. The wife's place was in the home, her husband and children were never far from it. When they went out, they went together, in carriage, or wagon, or sleigh. Their ambitions centered around the home-place, driving them to build a better house, to acquire more land, to achieve, as a family, higher standing in the community.

Doubtless father and mother felt affection for their children and loved each other, but in many families those other values were paramount.

## The Community Supported Family Life

Whether in town or country, the community of those years was stable and the people felt a strong sense of neighborhood which exerted a profound effect upon all. A distinguished gentleman who had refused a certain duty, changed his mind when he was solemnly asked, "What would the neighbors think?"

Especially did the neighborhood affect the family. Marriage was regarded by the community as the ideal for men and women. In several colonies bachelors paid a special tax; and an unmarried woman was a person to be pitied. To gain the full approval of the community one must get married. The community held the family together, regulated its life, and helped in the control and development of the children. If a husband or wife thought of separating, he or she would not only have to face the disapproval of the community, but would have to break the many ties that bound them together and forfeit the values they enjoyed in the family.

Suppose a man's wife were a termagant making his life a torment, or suppose the zest went out of his association with her. He could not leave the home into which he had put so many years of labor. He could not send her away, for he must have someone to keep house for him and perform the countless chores that fell to her lot.

Should her husband become cruel, or shameless in his conduct with other women, where could a wife go? To return to her own home would be only to assume the old state of bondage, and there was no other way by which she could support herself.

Always there would be the pressure of the community to keep them together, for they valued highly the good will of their neighbors, who were one in believing that marriage was a permanent relationship which should be broken only by death.

It is not strange that there were few divorces then. There were these cohesive forces holding husband and wife together, and the pressure of the community keeping them from breaking apart.

This picture of the family of the early days is overdrawn, one-sided; yet it gives a background against which we can see more clearly the family as we know it now.

## Social Changes Affecting These Values

Changes have taken place in the community and in the world in which the community is set, which have laid their hands upon the family to a considerable extent, and, in a measure, refashioned it. Let us examine them sketchily. They are interrelated and have developed together and, therefore, can hardly be looked at separately. We are concerned only with their impact upon the family.

The coming of the industrial age, the building of great cities, the mechanization of life, the emancipation of women, the new attitude toward children, the rapid shifting of people from one locality to another, especially from the country to the city, two major wars, our changed moral and religious ideals—all these have had their influence on the family.

Men and women no longer have to get married to escape from home. College opens its doors to many, and factory and office, store and filling station, offer them all a chance to make an independent living.

The family is not now a self-sufficient economic unit. Much that it needs cannot be made in the home, and if it can it may be bought more cheaply from Sears Roebuck, or at a bargain sale in a store downtown. The home is facetiously referred to as the place we put the things we buy.

The picture of the wife going to the spring for water, or drawing it from a well, belongs to yesterday. Today she turns a spigot and has a plentiful supply. She no longer laboriously fills lamps with kerosene and trims wicks; she pushes a button and there is light abundant. She does not now spend long hours boiling clothes in a great iron pot in the back yard, scrubbing them on a washboard, and ironing them with a nine-pound flat iron; an automatic washing machine, dryer, and ironer are at her disposal. It isn't surprising that when a woman of questionable age was trying to teach a group of present-day youngsters an old song, "This is the way we wash our clothes," going through the motions of a woman at a scrubbing board, they couldn't get it. They could, however, show her the way in which the tumblers worked in an automatic machine. Ninety-nine per cent of our urban homes, and eighty-six per cent of those in rural areas, rejoice in the blessings electricity brings. An electric refrigerator makes cutting ice from the pond unnecessary; an oil furnace replaces the open fire, and wood no longer has to be cut and hauled. A deep freeze, packaged foods, frozen meals, make housework simpler and easier. It isn't unthinkable that when a wife told her husband, "Dinner is a little burnt tonight," he replied, "What, don't tell me they had a fire at the delicatessen!" More seriously, a wife's work in the home may be reduced to a minimum by gadgets within, and special services from without, so that her husband may regard her as a consumer rather than a producer, a competitor for the common purse, especially if she has extravagant tastes.

Children have ceased to be an economic asset, and are now quite a financial liability. The use of machinery makes their work on the farm unnecessary. Small farms do not furnish support for more than one son, and we see the unending trek of young boys and girls to the city. In it there is no room for many children in the miniature house, or tiny apartment. Our families grew smaller and smaller until 1941 when we had the beginning of a "baby boom," which is still with us to the dismay of the prophets and of those responsible for our schools and colleges.

A child a financial asset! It is estimated, depending upon the socio-economic level, that it now costs from $5,000 to $30,000 to raise a boy until he is 18. When parents of the twentieth century become old they cannot expect their children to make a place for them in their limited quarters. They must seek asylum in homes provided for the aged by lodges, or State, or Church.

The present-day family doesn't minister to a man's ego, as did that of yesterday. He can no longer lord it over his wife, for she stands on a level with him; children do not bow low in his presence—not many have learned to honor their father.

Many of the functions belonging to the family of the colonial period have been taken over by outside agencies. Schools are closer at hand, and if they are distant, buses deliver our children to their doors. Many teachers discourage parents from helping their children at home, and the curriculum of the lower schools is so organized that most, if not all, of a child's work is done during school hours.

When in 1780 the modern Sunday school movement had

its beginning in Gloucester, England, and began to spread rapidly through the British Isles, some far-seeing Scotsmen voiced the fear that it might relieve parents of a sense of responsibility as it took over the task of the religious education of children. That fear has been realized in America. Father has abdicated the office of priest in the home, and Mother is too busy, it may be with church affairs, to teach the Bible to her offspring. The Sunday church school with its expanded sessions, the vacation church school, children's choirs, youth organizations, camps, and conferences seem fully able to care for the spiritual needs of our sons and daughters. Why should parents worry? There are so many other things to do! If the whole family goes to church its members sit anywhere but in the same pew.

Recreation isn't an affair of the united family today. We do not have to cudgel our brains to think up interesting things to do. All we need is money. As with everything else, we can buy our entertainment. Skating rinks, bowling alleys, moving picture theatres, sports of all kinds—golf, tennis, baseball, basketball, football—compete for our dollar. If families can afford a radio or television set—ninety-six per cent have a radio—they can have their amusement at home. The family doesn't go out together any more. Each follows his own interest. And in the home no two seem to want to hear the same program or look at the same telecast. The solution of the squabbles that develop in some homes is for each person to have his own radio, and it may come to that with television, so that every one apart from the others may listen or look.

The family is not the close-knit group that it was, held together by multiplied common values. Some of them, as we have seen, are gone and others are not existent to the same degree. The family is not now the career of its members. Each one has his own governing ambition. We are talking now of the "atomistic" family.

The strong sense of neighborhood is no more; though people in the city are often packed together like sardines, there is an anonymity, an impersonality, about the city which leaves them ignorant of the names of those who live next door, or across the street, or even alongside of them on the twentieth floor of a towering apartment house. The mobility of life in America, which might almost be symbolized by the trailer, keeps us from knowing those who live in our own block. It is estimated that four-fifths of those who get married change their living quarters at the time of marriage, or in the following year, and that after ten or fifteen years of marriage one-fifth move to another home each year. A man on a bus was overheard saying to his seatmate that they were in a new home each year, as his wife found it less trouble to move than to clean house.

The community's appreciation of marriage is not quite the same. A bachelor may not be condemned, but judged to be free and fortunate. An unmarried woman is not scorned as an "old maid," but referred to deferentially as a "career woman."

The neighborhood helps little with the proper rearing of children; often a mother's chief difficulty is with youngsters from nearby homes whose parents have ideals sharply at variance with hers. How often is the complaint heard, "But, Mother, Mary's mother lets her do this." From the parents' standpoint, the task of raising children would be easy if there were no neighbors!

A man wishes to be free from his wife's nagging. The house is rented, the furniture has been bought on the installment plan. Around the corner is a serviced apartment with its attractive coffee shop. Should he become sick he has hospitalization insurance. He can just pick up his hat and walk out!

A woman is tired of listening to her husband's faultfinding. She is not dependent upon him for support. She can go back to her old job, which paid almost as much as he is making, or more. It is easy to find a comfortable place to stay. She, too, can go her own way.

Neither feels the pressure of community disapproval, for there are no neighbors in the old sense. If there are neighbors whose judgment counts, they would hardly be inclined to condemn, for in almost every family connection there is a divorced person, and the climate of opinion has changed. People are not sure that God joined her to her husband, or that He means for this pair to stay together. The fact that Adlai Stevenson was nominated for the Presidency by the Democratic party in 1952, and that Sir Anthony Eden was made Prime Minister of England, are straws showing which way the wind of public opinion is blowing throughout Anglo-Saxon lands.

The family is not tied together by the same number of strong cords as held in our grandfathers' day; neither is there the same decided voice of a meaningful neighborhood commanding husband and wife to cleave to each other. Is it strange that the divorce rate in less than a hundred years has increased ninefold, and that it is much lower in rural areas which have not felt in the same way the impact of social changes?

## Love Remains

We hear so often the lament, "Divorce is destroying marriage!" But it is not divorce that has been destroying marriage. Divorce is not a cause, it is only a symptom, an evidence that something has been happening within the marriage relation through the past decades as a result of social changes.

Is marriage then to come to an end? Men and women will continue to marry for many reasons. It may be in part because, as Levy and Monroe say, "They lived in families as children and still cannot get over the feeling that being in a family is the only proper, indeed the only possible way to live."[2] As a matter of fact more people in the United States are getting married than ever before. About ninety-two per cent of all men and women in this country now marry, and the proportion of those marrying early is increasing.

Has marriage really deteriorated in its values? It has changed, yes, but potentially for the better. I am glad that my wife didn't have to come to me because she had nowhere else to go if she would be at all free, or protected from a world in which women are discounted, or in danger. I am happy that for her marriage was optional; that she chose me because in her freedom to marry or not she believed that life with me would bring the richest satisfactions and growth to us both, and enable us to serve our Lord better. I rejoice that she is not a chattel whose person and goods are mine, a drudge to perform menial tasks at my bidding, the bearer of children at my will to add to the corps of workers on the farm. I am glad that she is my companion whom I honor and love, with whom I share some of the household duties as she shares with me the burden of my work. I am grateful that children are brought into the world because we want them for themselves, and for the contribution they can make to Christ's Kingdom; and that the intimate relationship which means their birth is not solely for that purpose, or a matter of shame or fear, but an experience of a true oneness of life, a sacramental act, which results in mutual joy, the growth of love, the enrichment of our personalities.

We can rejoice together that our children are not just another set of employees upon whom we can impose our desires, nor robots who obey because it is ours to command; but persons who through our joyous fellowship together love us as we love them, who can freely discuss and see the Christian ideals we hold for them and which, perhaps wisely modified, they now hold as their own.

The value of this companionship and affectional relationship is becoming more evident as other values are diminished. In the strain and loneliness of life in the city, where competition for position and possessions is so strong and unremitting, where the isolation of people is so real and true friends are so few, in a day when the future seems so uncertain, men and women need for their own happiness and sense of security their love for each other and for their children. And children are lost without families in which love dwells.

Many are realizing that love is the primary value in marriage, seen more clearly because the other functions, economic, reproductive, protective, recreational, educational, and religious are not so insistently before them.

While some of these functions remain, though in a somewhat different way, and in their exercise understanding and love deepen, the central value of marriage today is love, the fellowship through which a man and a woman, alike yet dissimilar, experience a satisfaction and a development, a service to the world, which they could not know alone or in any other relationship. This will abide, because it meets so deep a need social changes cannot destroy it.

Dr. Burgess, of the University of Chicago, is sure that America is turning toward companionship marriage. He feels that if a marriage survives it will be the result of the strength of the interpersonal relations of its members, as manifested in affection, rapport, common interests and objectives.[3]

This must be clearly understood if men and women are to prepare themselves successfully for marriage today; for the choice of a life-partner, for mutual growth in the relationship which is a symbol of the relationship of Christ and His Church.

# Love and Marriage

*I*F FAMILY LIFE TODAY can be basically a deep and lasting friendship, the richest, most creative that life knows, in which individuals are kept together not by neighborhood pressure, nor their needs created by an older culture, but largely by the Christian love that belongs to such a relationship, does it not follow that those who contemplate marriage should realize this and do some solid thinking before they marry?

That marriage should be a high and permanent friendship does not mean that there is no place for romance in it, nor that sex does not have its part. There is a place for the cardiac-respiratory reaction. It is natural for the heart to beat faster when a boy and girl who are in love are together, but when the heart says, "yes," the head should cry, "amen." The head can speak no such word with wisdom unless real thought has been given to the meaning of this relation.

America is plagued today by the conception that romantic love is the supreme qualification for a successful marriage. The idea that there is one man for one woman, who will immediately recognize each other when they meet, is kept before us by magazines, motion pictures, television programs, soap operas, and national advertising. All these indicate that such love overcomes all differences in age, culture, education, and religion, and makes up for any shortcomings in either individual.

> "Out of the fog came a girl,
> Out of the clouds came a man,
> Out of their meeting came romance."[1]

But romance is not enough. A boy may put a halo about the head of his dream girl. For her he may be a glamorous knight riding out of the West. But the fog lifts, the clouds blow away, and the boy and girl see each other in the disillusioning light of everyday living in a bandbox of a house. A few looks are enough, and marriage which had no basis on reality comes to an unhappy end.

If young people could be convinced that marriage is a friendship which depends for its fulfillment on the true character of the persons involved, they might heed the late Hugh Black's earnest warning against "drifting" into such a relationship. If he had been writing today he might have added, "on the stream of romantic love."

Years ago a girl and I asked each other the question, "Why do two people like each other?" Our combined enthusiasm for friendship, aided a bit by a full moon, provided this answer: You like a person first, because of what he is in himself; second, because of what he does for you; third, because of what you do for him; and fourth, because of what you do together.

I have taken our conclusion, reached in the long ago, before literally thousands of people in conferences and discussion groups and it has stood the test. I do not mean that everything about this relationship is easy to understand—Montaigne in his essay on Friendship in speaking of his close friend, Etienne de La Boétie, said, "If you ask me why I love him, I can only answer, because it was he, because it was I."[2]

There is mystery in friendship. But these conditions of a true friendship will bear study.

## I. We Love a Person Because of What He Is in Himself

A woman in the beginning may be drawn to a man by his physical appearance. He is so clean, so strong, so handsome. A man may find a woman attractive because of her fresh beauty, her slim figure, her smart-looking clothes. This is natural, and does not end after their first association. Joy comes through a proper pride in the looks of another.

Terman, in his *Psychological Factors in Marital Happiness*, finds that carelessness of wives in personal appearance is a major cause of marital unhappiness.[3] Wives likewise complain of husbands, "They slump," "They get seedy," "A three days' stubble of beard is not any more attractive to me than cold cream on my face is to him." These are small things. But seemingly trivial matters can irritate and lead to increasing tension.

The pattern of boy and girl fellowship in the United States —dating, going steady, informal understanding, private engagement, with parents and best friends in on the secret before its announcement—is good. If followed, it gives both an opportunity to look below the surface for qualities of mind and heart which will appeal now and will make their relation increasingly joyous and rich to the end of life. Unfortunately too many are caught in our speed-mad age and get married before they really know each other. Judges of Domestic Relations courts tell us that "precipitous marriage" is one of the primary reasons for so many marital failures.

There is real danger that a boy and girl may be with each other often, over a long period of time, and yet experience no mutual self-revelation because they are almost always with a crowd, or so busy doing something, or watching something that there is no chance for the kind of conversation and experience that open heart to heart.

Anyone who has had any close association with young people who are seriously considering marriage has been asked many times, "How can we know we really love each other and that our love will last?"

The interesting-looking check lists in popular magazines provide no real answer. Thoughtful books can give only helpful guidance. One cannot know with certainty. He can only build up probabilities that point to a particular person, then act on them, and in the actual experience of marriage have his faith validated.

## QUALITIES TO LOOK FOR AND DEVELOP

There are, however, certain characteristics in another for which one should look, and which he himself should possess if true love is to begin on a sure basis.

1. *Integrity* stands at the forefront.

Jesus speaks of the happiness of the pure in heart. There is much more in this word than chastity, a heart clean of unholy interest in, or desire for, another. The very soul must be free from all dissembling. It demands honesty, an incapacity for deception, a strong alliance between thought and word and will.

Sincerity is at the basis of any true friendship, for how can one know another unless there is a real correspondence between what he says and does and what he is? How can one trust another unless he can believe in him?

A humble shoemaker, whom Calvin Coolidge was happy to claim as his friend, was asked what he understood friendship to mean. He replied, "A condition of perfect trust." Hugh Black, that brilliant preacher, makes trust the "first requisite" for friendship. They are so right.

Trust frees one person from suspicion, jealousy, and lifts the other to the level of his friend's trust in him. A wife who trusts doesn't have to phone her husband, or have him phone her during the day, so that she may check on where he is and what he is doing. She doesn't have to make him account for every minute of the day when he comes home. A sergeant said to his chaplain on their way back from France, "I am coming back to my wife just as I left her—clean." Her trust in her husband delivered her from anxiety while they were separated, and inspired him to be true to her.

2. *Loyalty* is essential.

Josiah Royce in his *Philosophy of Loyalty* maintains that loyalty is "the heart of all the virtues."[4] It is central in friendship. There must be the utter devotion of two people to each other. The classic definition of marriage stated by Lord Penzance in 1866, "the voluntary union for life of one man and one woman to the exclusion of all others," agrees with this ideal. Paul, resting his thinking on the Old Testament and the words of our Lord, would support it; for his charge to husbands is that a man leave his father and mother and be joined to his wife, and they two shall be one flesh.[5] By implication this is also his word to wives. Their primary loyalty is to each other. Mothers and fathers must take second place. If parents are wise they will be glad that in marriage their children put the husband or wife first; for they must know that the new family will be in jeopardy if the ties that bind husband and wife to their parental homes are stronger than those which hold them to each other in the home they have just created.

While it is unselfish love that should prompt father and mother to take their hands off of the lives of their children, it is this freeing attitude that will win for them the deeper, growing love of the young family, and a better opportunity to help, should help be needed. A part of our changing culture is the establishing of the new home apart from the old.

The birth of a child does not break the primary loyalty of husband and wife to each other. They will love this blessed little boy or girl devotedly, but each is still first in the heart of the other. Only so can they build a family in which children can be truly happy. For if one or the other parent gives a child the primary place, tension develops between father and mother and the peace of the home is gone.

While the man must give time and strength to his business or profession, and the woman must have friends and interests outside the home, she is really first to him, and he to her. No matter how busy they are, they will make time to be together.

3. *Reverence* is necessary.

Each partner to the marriage is a person, not a creature, a thing, or an it, but a soul made in the image of God, unique, free. Each has a different heredity, a different family background, perhaps a different cultural experience and training. Each grew without knowing the other for fifteen or twenty years, or more. Each must, therefore, respect and rejoice in the other's individuality, grant him the right and freedom to be himself.

We have a tendency to think that when another differs from us in any way he is wrong, and our impulse is to make him over so that he will be like us. As surely as we attempt that, both of us are in trouble. Differences should not be a source of friction but a means of development as each stimulates the other to new viewpoints, fresh outlooks on life.

Count Keyserling is sure that in all permanent marriage the secret of lasting companionship is the art of growth through difference.[6]

Reverence should mean that neither should smother, or absorb, or dominate the other. In this day of independent womanhood the authoritarian husband has no place.

Perhaps reverence means a degree of privacy for each. Intimacy can be overdone in our tiny apartments. The very word "flat" has a sinister suggestiveness. In the old home in

Charleston, South Carolina, where I grew up, my father, a minister, had his study on the first floor, Mother had her sewing room on the third, and our common life was carried on on the second. There must be moments when each can be alone with himself and with God.

4. *Unselfish love* is basic.

It should be unnecessary to use this qualifying word, but there is the kind of love that demands rather than gives, that possesses rather than frees, that takes for granted rather than appreciates.

A young man on the verge of marriage said to me, "I want to give her something just because I love her." Love is imaginative, and sees things to do to which the loveless heart is blind. Another man in love, older and a little more thoughtful, wrote, "I feel like giving myself for her." Implied in the giving of himself was the purpose to make that self richer. True love seeks to give and to have something worthy to offer; to give without asking anything in return.

True love will not hold too close, will not be too possessive in its demands. It will not only allow, but encourage the other to seek interests outside of the home. Each, therefore, will find something fresh and valuable to add to the fellowship, like bees bringing back to the hive honey gathered from many lovely flowers.

5. *Emotional maturity* is indispensable.

Dr. Paul Popenoe says, "If there is a universal formula for success in marriage it is in two words, emotional adulthood." The Family Service Association of America looks at the other side, and puts highest on the list of usual causes for the breakdown of marriages, "the general immaturity of people marrying."

A child may have two ways of meeting a situation—temper

or tears. He falls over a chair and weeps so that another may run to comfort him; or kicks the chair or the cat in his fit of anger. It may be that his mother encourages such action by saying, "Bad old chair; kick the chair."

As he grows older, if he is maturing, he doesn't cry when he has an accident. A wise mother has not come on the run. He does not kick the chair, for his mother has enabled him to see that that isn't the way out of his difficulty. He has learned to accept his carelessness, or another's, and to determine to be more watchful in the future. He sees that he must face himself and his situation calmly and thoughtfully and come to some rational solution.

Some children just become older without growing up, or under sudden stress revert to their early ways of behavior. Many have an overcharge of fear or temper—they lie close together—for civilized life. They face a serious blocking of a major desire or a series of minor thwartings, and anger builds up until they must relieve it in some way.

A salesman loses a big account to a competitor, or is "called on the carpet" by his manager, or is subject to a myriad trifling annoyances. His bitterness grows and grows. He can't take it out on his customers or boss. There is no cat convenient, so he bottles it up inside and starts home. In all innocence and eagerness his wife opens the door, to have his stored-up wrath poured out upon her unsuspecting head. For him she is the cat, and figuratively speaking, he kicks her.

Reverse the picture. A woman is at home all day. Everything goes wrong. A fuse is blown somewhere so the vacuum cleaner won't work, and the electric iron is dead. She decides to go to the A. and P. and get the week's supply of food, only to find after she has struggled to the checking counter that she has left her purse at home. It is just "one of those days." That evening her husband blithely enters the house and cheerfully announces that all has gone well at the office. Thunder and lightning play about the bewildered man and may strike. If their bad days synchronize, or either responds to anger with anger, the neighbors may have to send for the police. How many books warn against both getting mad at the same time!

Look at the husband for a moment. It may be that to "blow off" will relieve the tension that is almost unbearable. There may be times when a little boy just has to kick the chair. If his wife can only be understanding and calm—not patient in an irritating way—can keep silent without any hint of condemnation in her attitude, listen quietly so that he can talk out the day's happenings, like a summer thunderstorm his unhappy feelings may blow away in a little while, and the atmosphere be all the more refreshing.

Humor may save the situation. One man tips his hat over the wrong side of his head to warn his wife that he has had a hard day so that she may make allowances for his bad humor. She in turn, if all has not been well, makes her plea for understanding by turning her apron wrong side out.

If the man is feeling inferior, insecure, the last thing for his wife to do is to blame him for losing a sale, or for being criticized by the higher-ups. He is discouraged enough already, fear was part of the heavy charge in his temper. What he needs is the assurance of a deep and lasting love, honest words of encouragement. It was a wise wife who made a careful list of what her husband had achieved during the past year, not only of what he had done in business but also the helpful things he had done for her and the children, and showed it to him when he was in the depths.

Married life would be so much happier if both husband and wife could understand themselves and each other better, and realize how often their tension-producing conduct is not deliberate but a holdover from their own childhood association with their parents. Very often unreasonable behavior, emotion that is greater than the apparent cause, is the result of early experience.

If in the home of one the husband dominated the wife, and in that of the other the wife was the master, you can see the difficulty that will develop when two young people from such different family backgrounds start building their own home. When children come, the question of discipline may add to the strain of living together, if in his home the children were under stern control and in hers they were allowed large freedom.

Differing attitudes toward money may create serious friction. If she grew up in a home where every penny was pinched twice before it was spent, and in his home there was a happy-go-lucky attitude, "easy come, easy go," being the motto, it is understandable that money for them could be the root of all kinds of evil.

He can't see why she wants to continue to work after they are married. His mother never did; to her it would have been unthinkable, a reflection on her husband. But her mother worked before the children were born and after the youngest started to school. She found joy in it and her husband and the children appreciated the comforts the added income enabled them to buy—the car, the television set.

A man marries a girl in part because of the way she smiles; a gesture, a turn of expression reminds him of his mother. Then he wishes her to be like *his* mother in other ways, and is disappointed because she is more like *her own* mother. On the other hand, his eyes are like her father's, and the wave in his hair; so she is unhappy later when he has to be himself and she can't fashion him into the likeness of the one to whom she was so devoted as a little girl.

Both husband and wife, out of their own early experience, have developed a self-image or ideal, and the role each is to play in marriage. Each has to look at the other and at life through his own eyes, which see what is already in his mind and heart. The husband and wife who are emotionally mature, who can face life at all rationally, realize that both are conditioned by their past. Each asks the question, "Why?" about his own conduct and the other's. The husband understands that his wife takes an attitude different from his toward some subjects and holds it, not because she is unintelligent or mean, or just plain stubborn, but because long years of living before they met have made her what she is. It will be hard for her to change, it will take time; probably in most respects she should not change.

Then he interrogates himself. And if he is wise and honest he may find that the ideas which in his own life he thought were so rationally grounded, are after all prejudices or habits which grew almost unconsciously out of the give-and-take of life in his home and his neighborhood group. As he thinks about their new life together he may be more and more ready to see that he is the one who needs changing, and more willing for her to continue as she is. As she too becomes mature she will be increasingly inclined, and able, to adjust to him and to their common life. It is as each understands himself and his life partner, the reasons lying back of what they are and do, and accepts himself and the other, that the adjustments needed can be wisely and happily achieved.

The mature person will not expect perfection in marriage. Someone has said that there are American wives who look for the perfection in a husband which an Englishwoman hopes to find only in her butler. Each should understand that the other is human, with the shortcomings and foibles that belong to our humanity. If one were perfect his life might be a constant condemnation, and any suspicion that he thought himself wholly righteous would make life with him almost unbearable.

The mature person sees the small fault, the momentary disagreement, even the violent quarrel, in the light of the real meaning and value of marriage, the deep-lying purpose to make it successful. Set in such a perspective it loses its power for serious hurt and, like the irritating grain of sand in the oyster, if rightly dealt with may result in something of real beauty and value.

Let us go back for a moment to Josiah Royce. His emphasis is on loyalty to a *cause*, to values beyond oneself, to something higher than a particular person; to an overarching principle that commands us, even "loyalty to loyalty."[7] If he were discussing marriage he would see something above each party in marriage to which both can give their all. Morgan and Morgan have something like this in mind when they raise the question with those contemplating marriage, "Do you feel there must also be some goal or cause larger than the marriage alone to which both parties are committed?"[8]

Psychiatrists unite in emphasizing that all is not well with man, and that his chief difficulty in developing the kind of personality that would enable him to live in harmony with himself and with others is with his own self, his ego. The Bible long ago centered man's difficulty here. Pride is held up as the major sin, setting oneself over against God, above anyone or anything else. Jesus calls us to deny self, to break its power over us. He sees that it is self that creates our problems in human relations, that alienates us from each other, separates us from God.[9]

Thoughtful people have realized this when they have sought for the cause of the tensions developing in their marriage. Many couples have confessed to the counselor, "We see our trouble now—we are both selfish." In marriage, perhaps as nowhere else, when two strong egos are brought together in close and constant contact the stage is set for self-assertion. Friction develops and serious harm may result for both. It is the hurt we do people through our own selfishness, and the isolation that comes from putting self over against God, that create our awful sense of loneliness, the deep sense of guilt that will not let us rest.

It is a dark picture of human nature that psychiatrists, Scripture, and our own consciences combine to draw. We are all in desperate straits—not just those who get married; we are sick with a malignancy that is apparently incurable. We need something to which self can surrender and in doing so can become humble and worthy. We need a healing sense of forgiveness that leaves the whole heart clean and free. We need a new feeling of unity with our fellows and with the universe in which our lot is cast, deliverance from our sense of aloneness. We need to love and be loved.

How can these needs be met? Where shall we turn? To whom shall we go? It is when we are utterly hopeless that we hear Christ saying, "Come unto me." It is through Him that we learn that "God is love"; that He loves us not because we are attractive, or good, or worthy in any way, but because it is His nature to love. He loved us when we were sinners and enemies; when we went our own way, indifferent to Him, or willfully violating His laws written in our own natures and in His world; when we worshiped only self. While our fellows may see in us things to admire as they look at our "outward appearance," the Lord "looketh on the heart." [10] He knows what is inside, what we have revealed to nobody else and have hardly admitted to ourselves. He sees it all and yet loves us, and wonder of wonders He desires and invites our love. Even if we can't love Him as He deserves, even if we do not respond, He loves us. His love is an unconditioned love, an inviolable love. Isn't this what Scripture means by grace—unmerited favor? As one of my Seminary professors put it, "Grace is infinite love for the infinitely undeserving." This is the source of our redemption. This is the Gospel—the Good News!

He forgives fully, everything—past, present, and future. His forgiveness reaches the most obscure, remote corner of our hearts. Every little spite, or fear, or meanness is forgiven, forever. His forgiveness is all-encompassing and final.

Such forgiveness, even to so great a love, is not simple and easy, a matter of the wave of a hand. In some way, beyond our understanding, when "all we like sheep" had gone astray, and "turned every one to his own way . . . the Lord . . . laid on him the iniquity of us all."[11] Turning from the Old Testament to the New, we hear Peter say, speaking of Christ, He bore our sins "in his own body on the tree,"[12] and, we reverently add, in His own heart. It is in our sinfulness, and the cost to Him of our redemption, that we see the immeasurable love of God. John puts it before us in those sublimely simple words, "God so loved the world, that he gave his only begotten Son, that whosoever believeth in him should not perish, but have everlasting life."[13]

To a God who loves like that, self surrenders. A humble pride grows—not in what one is or does as others see him and praise him; but in the fact that God loves him, forgives him, accepts him, with all his sins, his inabilities, his limitations. If God thus regards him it is enough. He can in all gratitude and lowliness of spirit know that he is a person of dignity and worth and can accept himself as he is. He no longer has to hide himself from himself for fear he will lose respect for himself. He no longer has to pretend to be better or wiser than he is because of his need to have his ego bolstered by the good opinion of others. He no longer has to try to impress people. He no longer has the feeling of inferiority that compels him to build up his ego by having to think that anyone who differs from him is wrong, by finding it necessary to win every argument, by insisting on having his own way in matters of no moment, by beating others at everything he undertakes.

To use a word heard so often today, nothing *threatens* him. Because he has already seen himself as he is, and accepted himself as God has accepted him, he does not fear exposure. Because he is everlastingly secure in God's redeeming love no one can make him feel inferior or afraid.

Because he has accepted himself with all his own faults and incapacities he can accept others. Because God has forgiven all that he is, all that he has done and left undone, he can forgive others, with no vitiating feeling of self-righteousness or superiority in his attitude, for he is a sinner too. He does not resent mistakes, nor anger, nor slights, nor other injuries—he forgives.

One with God now; through God's own life, which is in him, he is united to his fellows with a bond that nothing can break. He is bound to them as they are bound to him, by their common loyalty not just to each other but to God. He can love them and they him because God loves them and His love is in them.

We have gone far afield from the home, but all that has been said bears on the exacting life of a man and a woman together. For the emotional maturity they both need comes

finally from understanding and accepting themselves as they
see themselves in God's sight, and know they are accepted of
Him. Because they accept themselves they can accept and bear
with each other. Because they have been forgiven they can
forgive each other. Because they are loved with a love which
fills their hearts they can love each other devotedly and to the
end.

What I have expressed as an ideal we do not find in many
groups, even churches, nor in many homes. But as we yield
ourselves more and more to the love of God revealed in Christ,
will not Paul's hope for the Philippian church more and more
be fulfilled in our churches and in our homes? "Be like-
minded," he says, "having the same love, being of one accord,
of one mind. Let nothing be done through strife or vainglory;
but in lowliness of mind let each esteem other better than
themselves." [14]

It is in Christ that we find best exemplified the qualities
necessary in husband and wife for their richest life together.

*Integrity*. Christ's yea was always yea and His nay, nay.
When His life was at stake He swore to His own hurt and
changed not.[15] His disciples, when they really knew Him after
His resurrection, trusted Him to the death.

*Loyalty*. His close friend denies Him. He holds to him,
sends him a special message on the morning of His resurrection, and later restores him to the fellowship. "Having loved
his own . . . he loved them unto the end." [16]

*Reverence*. Persons are sacred to Him. He *calls* His disciples, He does not *force* them to follow Him. He does not
pour them into a single mold, reduce them to a common de-
nominator. He allows the rich young ruler to make his own
choice, to go his own selfish way. One of the wonders of life
is that God leaves us free, even to sin.

*Love.* One word is enough, "Greater love hath no man than this, that a man lay down his life for his friends."[17]

Paul, in the thirteenth chapter of First Corinthians, is drawing a portrait of love as he glimpsed it in Christ. As we sit before it, it torments us, its loveliness is our despair. But we are not called upon to strive to copy line by line in our own lives what we see in it. We are rather to find there a spirit which takes hold of us.

I urged a young couple who were in serious difficulty to steep their very souls in that chapter until they should begin to feel in themselves the love it pictures. It might be well for us all to do this, with Henry Drummond's classic, *The Greatest Thing in the World*, as our guide. As this is done, realizing that we are in reality looking at our Lord, something will happen within us.

Drummond is also the author of *The Changed Life*.[18] In this thin book he tells of the way in which the stars impress their glory on the photographic plate in a great telescope which is fixed steadily on them, and affirms that if we keep looking at Christ something of His beauty will become ours. In part this will be due to the operation of a natural law. That to which we give our attention day by day becomes real to us and strongly influences us. But there is more to our experience with Christ than that. It is not just through our humble contemplation of Christ that we become like Him. God is at work in us. Something deeper is happening than known psychological processes can explain. Paul is sure of this, for he says, "We all, with unveiled face, beholding the glory of the Lord, are being changed into his likeness from one degree of glory to another"; and adds, "for this comes from the Lord who is the Spirit."[19]

The transformation may be slow, we may be inclined to discouragement because a day's growth is so small. But the result is sure. Little by little He becomes the compelling center of our lives, and our ambitions and our purposes are unified and lifted in Him, because the Holy Spirit is at work in us. With our eyes fixed on Him, we take the long view and see our values and everyday happenings in the light of eternity.

Through our devotion to Him another problem of married life is solved. The question is raised in many books, should the family have one head or two, and which should be the head? The solution for the Christian is found in the attitude of a family about which the father tells this story: "One day a neighbor's boy, describing to my son an argument his father and mother had staged the night before, said, 'My mother is boss in our home. Who is boss in your home—your father or your mother?' With hardly a moment's thought, my son said, 'God is boss in our home.' " If God is really the head of the home, no question will be raised about which of the other members is superior. On the inner side of wedding rings worn by a husband and wife who had lived joyously together for many years was an inscription which explained the richness of their fellowship, "Each for the other, and both for Christ."

We have here a picture of a Christian home. For the home is Christian when husband and wife put Christ first, and love each other with a love which fellowship with Him inspires and fosters—a love intelligent, unselfish, enduring. Such a love will not end with the family, it cannot be confined to the home, it will move out into the community in blessing and be concerned for the ends of the earth. The Christian home is the best human illustration of the meaning of Christian love. It is the basis and hope of the spread of that love throughout the world.

We have spent so much time on the first reason why one person loves another because it is fundamental. If each is the kind of person who elicits love, the rest follows, and love rests on an unselfish basis. We love, not to get something, but because the other deserves our love, and we deserve his.

Let us now look more briefly at the other reasons why we love another person.

## II. We Love a Person Because of What He Does for Us

This seems selfish and would be dangerous to consider apart from what already has been said about love because of what another is in himself. We love another for himself; but what he does for us as an expression of the love he feels adds to our love for him. The numberless thoughtful acts, the unexpected gifts that cost thought rather than money, which are a part of the days of courtship draw the heart of a girl to a man.

If love which in part is born of such kindnesses is to grow, they must be continued. Not just the same things probably, but others which are different and more meaningful because they are prompted by a love which has become more understanding and inventive through its development.

A woman said to a friend, "My husband would die for me but he always forgets to pass me the salt. Now he may not have a chance to make the great sacrifice, but I need the salt three times a day." Suppose that years before he had saved her life at the risk of his own when they were on a trip shortly after their marriage. One night he struggled awake to find the hotel room filled with smoke, and his wife overcome by it. With a wisdom and a strength and a courage he could never explain, he wrapped her in a blanket, fought his way through the murky, flame-filled hall and carried her down the fire escape to waiting, friendly arms. For months the severe strain on a weak heart put a question mark over his life. How much his wife would love him then because he had jeopardized his life to save hers.

Often we think that our love for another is determined by the value to us of what he does, and its cost to him. But that is not always true, and one supreme act of devotion is not sufficient for all the years of life together. The wife in our story might have found it difficult to keep her love for her husband growing through reliving in her memory those ghastly days, if he had neglected her thereafter. She would need the passing of the salt, the small acts prompted by thoughtfulness and affection which make the days easy and happy. Drummond says, "Love is courtesy in little things."[20] Love sees the multiplied opportunities for helpfulness that each day brings, and acts.

So often love stops growing because marriage seems to be the death of the kind of attention the wife received before the honeymoon ended, the careful consideration of her wishes. How many wives complain, "He leaves things around," "he spills ashes on the rug," "he is late for meals," "he doesn't seem to know the struggle I have to keep things hot," "he blames me if the food is cold," "he never brings me anything," "he never takes me anywhere," "he forgets our anniversaries," "he takes me for granted," "he doesn't praise me any more," "he never tells me that he loves me." This list is long and it could be made much longer. Most of the things done and not done are not big things, and cost little except thoughtfulness. It is not the big things that count most. Mrs. Wendell Willkie confessed that her husband sometimes in the rush of his crowded life forgot a birthday, or a wedding anniversary; "But," she added with a happy smile, "that is not important. What is important is how he treats you every day." Dr. Bowman wisely observes, "Figuratively speaking, marriages that fail seldom 'go on the rocks,' as is commonly said. They are more likely to be wrecked on piles of sand—the combined and cumulative effect of numerous contributing factors, no one of which alone would be sufficient to produce failure."[21]

Wives need praise now and then, the sincere expression of love. There is a place for the right kind of romance in marriage. I must admit to reading and enjoying "Blondie," and have been encouraged by the fact that Witty and Lehman found that while only eighty-three per cent of average children, with an IQ of 90 to 110, read the comic strips, one hundred per cent of those with an IQ of over 140 read them! I commend one of Chic Young's cartoons to husbands. Blondie is knitting, Dagwood is hidden, except for a bit of hair on end, behind the newspaper. "Dagwood, do you think I am beautiful and look younger every day?" "Yes, dear!" "Do you love me?" "Yes, dear!" "Well, why don't you tell me these things without my asking you?" The last panel shows an astonished man looking at an irate wife. But if Dagwood had been understanding would he have been astonished? Would the tense situation ever have developed? Men need to heed Mark Twain's admonition: "Try complimenting your wife even if it does frighten her at first."

Especially does the wife who is a true homemaker need appreciation and encouragement. She doesn't keep the chickens, or raise vegetables, or make the children's clothes as in the old days; but despite all the gadgets at hand she often works hard. Not long ago I addressed a group of women, and contrasted sharply the colonial woman on a farm with the city wife in the age of technocracy, implying that the latter had little to do. At least two of them, with calloused hands, came up afterward to take me to task. They were justified. If their work in the home had been paid for by the hour, it would have had high monetary value. Often the wife whose interest and work center in the home, needs to be helped toward an appreciation of what she is doing. When in a crowd where other women are talking about their interesting careers, she feels a bit inferior as she confesses that she is "only a housewife and mother." Her husband should help her see that hers is the greatest career in the world. We should have some word with rich overtones which would reveal that she is the creator of life, the transmitter of our moral and spiritual heritage, the inspirer of today's leaders, the determiner of the nation's tomorrow.

How can a woman's love for a man grow unless he does those things for which her heart hungers? Though they may not be necessary for physical well-being, they mean more to life than bread and meat. The secret of the growth of love and joy in married life is in the thoughtful expression of love in daily living. A story told of Mrs. Dwight Morrow illustrates this. Shortly after her twentieth wedding anniversary, seated next to Paderewski at dinner, she recalled to the great pianist the night long ago when she had first heard him play, in the Northampton Academy of Music.

"Do you often go back to your alma mater?" asked Paderewski.

"Yes," replied Mrs. Morrow. "I like to sit in my old chapel seat and think how much happier I am now than I ever thought I should be."

Paderewski was deeply interested. "Do you mean to tell me you are happier now than you ever expected to be when you were eighteen?"

"Yes, indeed," she replied.

"Mrs. Morrow," he exclaimed with a low bow, "please permit me the honor of meeting your husband!"[22]

What is true for the woman is true for the man. His heart needs nourishment as well as hers. He needs the challenge of her expressed love and trust to be worthy. Thirty years ago Judge Joseph Burke of the Court of Domestic Relations in Chicago, out of his experience with the 35,000 who made complaints in court each year, worked out a list of ten commandments for husbands and wives in the hope that this overwhelming stream of unhappy people might be moderated. One of them, to wives, was, "Tell him that he is the world's greatest husband and he will be." It is not so easy as that, but if she can begin to believe it, it will help.

To a class I was teaching about the Christian family the question was put, "What do you really want of marriage?" Part of the answer in one paper is worth quoting, "First a *good* husband. I feel too deeply about Frank to know how to put it into words. He is the best Christian I have ever known, in the *true* sense of the word. There's no substitute for *plain everyday goodness*, and that's Frank!" How could a man whose wife felt that way about him fail to respond?

Life for the man is not easy. Whether he works with his hands or head, is a day laborer or in an office or profession, there is the struggle to hold a job, or to get ahead; the pressure of more work than can be done. He needs the sustaining strength that only a good home can give. The president of the American Brake Shoe Company felt so keenly that a wife is the key to a man's success that he tried to get the wives of his employees to understand what their husbands were doing and help them by building a home in which they could find rest and joy and courage.[23]

Wherever you turn you find it is the wife who is behind the man's capacity for work. Dr. Alexander Whyte, meeting Principal Rainy of New College on an Edinburgh street, when the latter was under unusual stress, misrepresented and vilified, said, "I can't understand you. You seem as blissful and radiant as a child." "Oh, but Whyte, I am very happy at home."

As the wife does something for the husband and he does something for her, as they more and more depend upon each other for joy and inspiration, the love of each for the other will grow.

### III. We Love a Person Because of What We Do for Him

This is something we are apt to overlook. Benjamin Franklin said long ago in *Poor Richard's Almanac*, "He who has once done you a favor will be more ready to do you another than he whom you yourself have obliged." Franklin learned this principle through an interesting experience. He sought, without success, to secure the good will of the clerk of the Pennsylvania Legislature by doing him several favors. Then he wrote asking him for the loan of a rare book which he needed and could not get elsewhere. The book was sent at once. Franklin immediately read and returned it (note this fact), with an appreciative letter. The clerk, as a result of doing something for him, became his friend.

How clearly we see this in our relationship to a child. He can do nothing for us. It is as we do things for him that our love grows. It is often the sick child, the one who has the greatest need, the one for whom we do the most, that we love much, if not the most. This does not need to be illustrated further.

Some years ago when we were being surfeited with books describing the breakdown of the family in America, *What's Wrong With Marriage, The Bankruptcy of Marriage, The Drifting Home*, to name only a few, two young Ph.D.'s,

Binkley and Binkley, who had grown in their life together, wrote a book which they entitled *What Is Right With Marriage*. One idea from it has stuck in my mind, *There must be domestic activity and appreciation on both sides*.[24] Friendship cannot be a one-way relationship. The husband does something for his wife and she appreciates it. She does something for him and he appreciates it. If the experience is one-sided, there will be little or no growth. On the contrary, hostility may develop.

Life works that way in all of our relationships. A chief reason for the unhappy attitude toward the United States of the nations we are helping is that the relationship is one-sided, activity and appreciation are not mutual. The Netherlands ambassador, addressing a Richmond, Virginia, forum in 1952, made this clear. "We have," he said, "a poor relation complex, a feeling that we owe you too much." Cardinal Spellman, trying to offset this feeling, entitled an address he made in Belgium in 1953, "America, Grateful Child of Mother Europe," and began by saying, "What we give you is the payment of a debt."

It is frequently easier to do something for others than to have them do something for us; our miserable egos again! To help another makes us feel superior, to have him do something for us creates a feeling of inferiority. So in our selfishness we build a one-way relationship. Sometimes a wife may be so independent that she refuses to let her husband do anything for her; the reverse may be true. Such an attitude is not fair to the friendship. It inevitably blocks its growth.

It may be that such a relationship developed without either realizing how it came about. A woman complained bitterly to a friend, "Don won't do anything for me. He never so much as carries a chair into the house. He just sits and watches me do it." It all came about because she moved fast and her husband was deliberate. In the early days he could never get to the chair first, and she never waited for him. So he gave up. She feels his neglect now, and he suffers in his relation to her because he doesn't help. The self-sufficient, capable woman wonders why her husband doesn't love her more and can't understand why that "helpless female" seems so attractive to men. Husbands and wives must keep in mind that *there must be activity and appreciation on both sides.* A one-way helpfulness is bad for both and destructive of the friendship, and always there must be appreciation.

We are driven back again to the kind of person each is; a selfless, sensitive love will be ready to help, or be helped, and will always be grateful for what it has received, and be happy in serving.

## IV. We Grow in Our Love for a Person as We Do Things Together

It is true that as two people do things together, love grows. Through shared experiences they understand each other better, their common interests multiply, they have more to talk about. The center of their thinking shifts from I to we— there is a new "we-ness" about life. In such fellowship, there are activity and appreciation on both sides.

There are things *in the home* to do together. Even a more leisurely breakfast or dinner may mean much. "It is amazing," someone has said, "how one's outlook on life can be changed just by an unhurried drinking of a second cup of coffee, with the companionship of one you love."

Washing dishes is a revealing experience. A broken plate, even if it is an heirloom, can occasion self-control, provoke laughter, and add a bit to the cement that binds two people together. Christopher Morley writes with insight:

> "The man who never in his life
> Has washed the dishes with his wife
> Or polished up the silver plate—
> He still is largely celibate."*

Reading aloud to each other if their tastes are at all congenial, listening to great music if both appreciate it, looking at something good on television which both find interesting, can create new ties that hold heart to heart.

It is well at times for a man to leave his business problems at the office and for his wife to keep silent about the difficulties with a servant, the neighbors, or the milkman, that have ruined her day. But often problems will be seen more clearly and worked through more wisely, and household matters can be adjusted more quickly and more happily, if each can talk things out to a sympathetic listener.

Again and again when I have been called to a church or to another type of service, and have struggled without result to reach a decision, I have talked it over with my wife, and as she listened quietly, or asked an intelligent question, I have found my way toward an answer.

If there are children, playing with them together, listening to their joys and sorrows—the discovery of a robin's nest, the breaking of a much-loved doll, bathing them and putting them to bed as a common task, watching together by the bedside of one who is sick—all contribute to a new closeness and love.

Nothing can mean quite so much as simple worship together before children come, or after they have left the home. Dr. and Mrs. William Brown have written an almost ideal guide

* From *Poems*, by Christopher Morley, copyright, 1917, 1946, by Christopher Morley. Published by J. B. Lippincott Company.

for those just married, in *Your First Week Together*.[25] A poem, a few verses of Scripture, and a prayer for each day of that week will help any couple to begin and to continue to worship together. So far as I know there is no special booklet for the days when the children are gone. By then it should not be needed.

Our Lord said, "Where two or three are gathered together in my name, there am I in the midst of them."[26] These two, husband and wife, as hardly any other two can, have the assurance of His presence as they pray; for on them in a real sense rests the prayer life of the world.

There are *things outside of the home* to do together. Sometimes this takes more planning, more consideration and effort. By temperament he may like to be on the go, while she is happier at home, or she may like to run around, while he enjoys sitting in his big chair with the day's paper, or the *Saturday Evening Post*. He may come home bone-tired, while she, with the day comparatively free, is overflowing with energy. Or, he may have just turned a big deal and is eager to celebrate, while she, with everything going at sixes and sevens the whole day through, is exhausted and ready only to lie down, or wring her hands.

They may be interested in doing different things because of their different backgrounds. He may love outdoor sports, she may care only for the movies, or the theatre, or the club. Each must grant the other freedom, and yet be ready to share the other's interest now and then. The spirit of fairness must govern. A picture of a wife looking accusingly at her husband who is absorbed in watching his favorite pitcher, has under it, "I know marriage is give and take; but how do you figure four ball games to one concert?" It is just as easy to find a picture of a husband, half asleep or rebellious, sitting by a wife who is thrilled as she listens to a symphony, or a lecture on art. But each now and then should be willing to suffer with the other and to try to understand what interests him.

A husband comes rushing into the kitchen, so excited he can hardly speak. "I made a hole in one!" he finally shouts. "That's nice," comes his wife's calm comment; "now if you don't mind, please go to the corner and get a loaf of bread." He comes down out of the golfing clouds with a thud, and wishes for a group of understanding men who will rejoice with him in realizing the hope of a lifetime.

He may hurt his wife just as badly if he cannot respond to her enthusiasm if, after many years of fruitless effort, African violets suddenly decide to bloom for her. With only a little thought about the other's hobby, each could have appreciated the other's startling achievement.

In Terman's study, forty-four per cent of both husbands and wives who were happily married said it was essential to take their vacations together. Fifty per cent said it was advisable, yet that it was good occasionally for a man to go fishing or hunting with his cronies, and for a woman to spend a while with her friends in the country, or in a big city viewing fashion shows or the new plays, or visiting the museums. They might come back to find new zest in being together.

It is needless to say that it is a part of their life together to belong to a church and to attend its services regularly and to participate in its work. Unless a matter of principle is involved —and if there is, they should be doubly sure before they get married—they should be members of the same church. By no means should the wife always join with the husband. If possible they should think through this important matter and make their choice of a church before marriage. It was a wise and fair man who said to his bride-to-be during their courtship, "I'm a Methodist, but I have not been particularly interested in my church, and I know your church means much to you; so we shall join the First Presbyterian Church together as soon as we get back from our honeymoon."

These then are the laws of a growing friendship, of a happy and enriching marriage. We love a person because of what he is, so both are obligated to *be* and to *grow*. We love a person because of what he does for us, and what we do for him, so we must live for and help each other. We love a person because of what we do together; so we must share each other's interests and activities.

Dr. Roy Burkhart tells of a married couple who had recently celebrated their golden wedding anniversary. When he was visiting them a few years before that, the husband said in the course of the conversation, "Well, it will not be long until we are married fifty years, and still we are not in love." Says Dr. Burkhart, "I looked at him in surprise. His face was deeply serious. I turned to his wife and received the best-timed wink I have ever seen. I got the cue. Then the husband laughed. 'We are not in love, we are still climbing into it.' "[27] This old couple must have found and obeyed these laws.

Isn't it natural for us to turn for a moment to our relationship with Christ who calls us His friends?[28] Do not the same laws hold if we are to grow in this greatest of all friendships?

We love a person because of what he is in himself. We find all the qualities we count the highest coming to perfection and harmony in Christ. Yet there is no aloofness, no superiority, for love fills His heart, and He seeks only to serve. He cannot grow, so if our friendship is to grow we must be with Him in prayer, and subdue the low in us if we are to see the high in Him, and so be ready for a richer fellowship.

We love a person for what he does for us. Christ did die

for us, and through His death we have been reconciled to God. New life is ours now and forever. We love Him for the cost to Him and the value to us of His sacrifice. Our love will grow as we think about the meaning of redemption. But must not we turn to Him every day for the help we so sorely need if our hearts are to respond fully—for guidance as the road divides before us, strength as temptations press in, forgiveness when we fail, comfort in the days of disappointment and sorrow?

If we try to carry on apart from Him, we shall not only stumble and fall, be bruised if not broken; but we shall not be fair to the friendship—it will not grow.

We love a person because of what we do for him. Christ has left His lifework in our hands. The outcome of all for which He lived, and suffered and died and rose again, depended on His disciples and rests with us. "You shall be my witnesses,"[29] He said to them and says to us. As we stand against some evil in our community for His sake, as we give ourselves to some worthy cause, speak a good word for Him, just live the humble, brave, generous life in our group that would commend Him to others, especially if it costs us something, our love for Him will grow. Activity and appreciation are on both sides—He helps us and we are grateful. We serve Him and we hear His words, "Well done."

We love a person because of what we do together. Christ's promise is, "Go ye . . . and, lo, I am with you."[30] As we seek to help others we find that He is with us, supplying a wisdom and strength without which we would utterly fail.

How often Billy Graham tells the great throngs to which he preaches with such power, that it is not what *he* does that brings them together, and moves them to come to the front in repentance or rededication. *Someone* is with him and it is His power that redeems. So it will be with us, as in our humbler way we seek to serve another. We shall find our Lord standing by our side and in this fellowship of service our love grows.

The conditions of a growing friendship with Him are very simple. He meets them all. If our friendship with Him does not grow it is not His fault.

We may be sure that if we grow in our friendship with Him, our highest human friendship will grow also in richness and joy. In this we have the secret of truly happy marriage.

Marriage has been discussed first, and at such length, because in so many homes there are no children. In some, it will be years before children come. In others the children have come, and have gone to create their own homes, or to begin life in the Other World. In others, there will never be any children because husbands and wives have planned it that way, or because, though they long for children with all their hearts, they can never have them. The 1950 census reveals the surprising fact that 47% of the nation's households include no child or young person under eighteen.

A further reason for emphasizing marriage at the outset, is that in homes where there are children, the happy, devoted relationship of father and mother is essential for their welfare. It would be almost useless to talk to parents about how to raise their children, if they had not made a success of their own marriage.

# Love During the Critical Preschool Years

OHN FISKE, an American philosopher of note, wrote a little book in 1883 which he entitled *The Meaning of Infancy*. In it he marvels at the fact that it takes so long for the human offspring to mature and become independent as compared with the young of animals. It requires twenty-five years to educate a man, while a chick can shift for itself in as many hours, a kitten in as many days, a colt in as many weeks. If you go down the ladder of life instead of up you find the working bee making its way out of the egg, shaking itself for a second or two, and proceeding to take its place among the particular group of workers it was born to join. Or there is the butterfly as the cocoon bursts open, ready to disport itself in the glory of a sunshiny day.

The advantage seems to be with the lower orders of life; but as Fiske so clearly sees, that is only apparent. The reflexes and instincts which equip an insect or animal for immediate living are his doom. They are fixed and unmodifiable except within narrow limits. Because he is ready to do so much at the beginning he can do little more as life goes on.

The helplessness of a baby is his opportunity. His capacity to make varied rather than definite responses, prepares him for almost infinite development. To quote Dr. Fiske, "It can be shown that man's progressiveness and the length of his infancy are but two sides of one and the same fact. . . . It is babyhood that has made man what he is."[1] Dr. Arnold Gesell stresses this again and again.

It is the modifiability of the child and his amazing capacity for growth in these early years that excite our wonder, fill us with concern, and challenge us to do our best to guide his development along right lines.

We can realize the meaning and value of these first years, and our resulting responsibility for the child, only as we understand his growth during that period. It is determined by the maturing of the capacities with which he is endowed through his hereditary equipment, and the environment of persons and the material world in which he lives and moves.

The emphasis put on one factor or the other would depend on whether the writer was influenced more by the biological or sociological approach; most students today combine them and look at the child from the sociobiological viewpoint. Sometimes we speak of maturation—the development of the child according to the patterns laid down in the organism at conception; and learning—that which he acquires through contact with his environment, and is dependent on his maturing. Jersild illustrates the difference by the statement, "We note that a child has *grown* two inches in height since we saw him last and that he has *learned* to recite 'Jack and Jill.' "[2] In another environment Tommy would never have learned that particular poem. Though there was in him the drive to grow, he would not have grown that much unless he had been provided with proper food and care.

We cannot separate original endowment and environment in the growth of a boy except for discussion, and we have to keep in mind that he is always a unit within himself. Thought, feeling and will, body and mind, hang together. He cannot think accurately when he is undernourished, and a temper tantrum may leave him physically exhausted. According to Dr. Gesell, "The child always reacts as an integer."[3] It is the *whole* child in his *total* environment whom we must ever keep in mind, though for the moment in order to recognize his rapid growth before he goes to school we divide him into parts.

## His Body Grows

How small a newborn baby is, how limp, how helpless! How little strength he has, how few reflexes, how meager is his capacity for co-ordination! He may be able to raise his head from a pillow a few hours after birth; but he can't turn over, he can't sit up. He just lies there. He is completely dependent on older people if he is to live and grow.

But how quickly he learns to turn over, to sit alone, to crawl, to pull himself up, to stand alone, to walk holding mother's finger. Then he is on his own, and before we know it he runs and skips and jumps, and races away from us. He is on the go all day long, and many an athletic father attempting to do everything his son does during his waking hours, by nightfall is utterly exhausted.

Perhaps the simplest and quickest way to demonstrate the amazing rapidity of his growth is to look at his weight and height. At birth he weighs from six to eight pounds; this he doubles in six months, trebles the first year. When he is six he has multiplied his weight at birth by seven, for he weighs forty-seven or eight pounds. Unless something goes wrong with his glands, he will not in all the rest of his life multiply by seven his weight at six.

When he is born he is twenty and a half inches tall, or long, if you prefer. His growth is rapid the first two years—ten inches the first year, five inches the second, and by six he has more than doubled his height at birth; for he stands now forty-five or six inches tall. Not many will double that ever, to the distress of our basketball coaches.

## He Grows After a Definite Order and as a Whole

Brain cells, nervous systems, glands, bones, muscles all grow together. He can't stand until leg bones and back are strong enough to support his body, and his feet big enough to balance it. He has to walk before he can run, and the ability to jump with both feet off the floor is not his at once.

He grows as an individual and not exactly like the average boy whose height and weight achievements month by month and year by year are set before us in tables or diagrams. It is interesting to compare our child with "norms" but we must remember that he is not average. He differs from others at birth and has his own rhythm of growth. If we try to push him beyond his maturing we may discourage him, or make him afraid, or give him a feeling of resentment toward us. Wait a little, and when he is ready he will skip, or climb, or draw without our urging. We wish him to stand, or walk, before our friends' Sammy of the same age, or to be taller and stronger. But we mustn't condemn him or ourselves if he fails. He can be only himself.

His bodily health conditions his whole personality. We must see that he becomes a good animal. This means food and sleep and play of the right kind and in the proper proportion. It may be a now-or-never with teeth and bones and the development of the sense organs and neuromuscular co-ordinations.

Dr. Ligon, as he watches these little folks, sees the necessity of "something to make a noise with, something to smell, bright things to look at, soft things to touch, things to tear."[4] He needs big balls and blocks early as his larger muscles develop first, Daddy to romp with, and later, children of his own age with whom to play. If we deny him things and people his body suffers, and probably his whole outlook on life.

## His Mind Develops

As you hold a baby in the crook of your arm and look into his inscrutable face,

> "Hardly he seems a life at all,
>     Only a something with hands and feet;
> Only a feeling that things are warm,
>     Only a longing for something to eat."[5]

He has no long, long thoughts, no short, short ones—only a vague feeling of satisfaction and dissatisfaction. He has nothing to think with, for his brain hasn't developed as yet, and he has no time to think for he sleeps twenty of the twenty-four hours—unfortunately, for the ordering of our own lives, not consecutively. Yet how quickly he moves from an almost vegetative existence to an intelligent life.

Quite early he is able to *recognize* some thing or person as having been seen before. Strang reports that at six weeks a baby responds with satisfaction to being with his mother, and that a boy of twenty-four weeks recognized his grandfather after he returned from an absence of two weeks. Mrs. Fenton's boy, in the twenty-ninth week, put a piece of zweiback in his mouth immediately, when the first time it was offered him he shook it like a rattle, and got it in unintentionally.

How quickly he *recalls* what he has heard, and reproduces it. A two-year-old may recite a score or more of nursery rhymes, and I have looked into the face of a man who, when four years old, recited the Shorter Catechism!

He not only reproduces the things he has seen or heard; but he *colors* them, looks at them in a fresh light, combines them creatively into new patterns. The dew of the morning is in his eyes and he can see what our eyes blinded by the glare of noonday cannot behold.

A woman said to a little child starting out of his yard, "What are you doing?" "I'm going prospecting!" "What do you expect to find?" "On a day like this, you might find anything!" And so he might, as we well know from listening to children tell of their adventures as they come back from their tour of God's outdoors.

How vitally they participate in dramatic play! As I was crossing our campus one day I saw a group of children playing together and a three-year-older standing by herself some distance away. Thinking that she had been ostracized, as children can be terribly cruel, I turned to where she was, hoping to comfort her, and asked, "What are you doing over here?" "Oh," she replied, cheerfully, "I'm the maid and this is my afternoon off." And she *was* the maid.

Children create imaginary companions to compensate for their inability to compete successfully with other boys or girls, the neglect of parents, their lack of friends.

A worker with children has called down a curse upon those who lay a feather's weight upon the wings of a child's imagination. We do not want them to live in a world of fantasy. But children to play with, constructive things to do, wise conversation, will enable them to distinguish between fancy and reality. However, we must allow and encourage them to dream by reading them idealistic stories, giving them play materials with which they can create, introducing them to the wonder of God's world.

How soon *he begins to think*. Years ago I heard a woman who had no children of her own, but was rated an expert, say that small children couldn't reason. But with six children in our family whom I had watched at work and play, and whose questions I had tried to answer, I wondered.

What is reason but the capacity to solve problems, to make

intelligent choices, to observe and compare things or facts, and draw proper conclusions? Little children do that. Dr. Strang tells of a baby in his first year who was offered a cracker when he already had one in each hand. He hesitated, looked first at his hands, then at the proffered cracker. Finally he put one cracker in his mouth and reached for the third cracker. He had no ready-made responses with which to meet a new situation, so he had to reason it out. Could you have done better?

His eagerness for knowledge is shown by his wide-ranging *questions:* "Where does the wind go?" "Why can't I see two things with my two eyes?" "What is my chin for?" "If I went upstairs could God make it as if I hadn't?" All these are from four-year-olds, involving physics, anatomy, and theology!

We realize how marvelous has been his intellectual growth as we become aware of his mastery of our language. At first he had no language but a cry, and close observers of children in hospitals say they cannot even tell what he is crying about —fear, anger, or pain. But at a year he will probably have a vocabulary of three words, at two, 272, at four, 1,540, and at six, 2,562. These are what are called *active* words, those he can use. His passive vocabulary, words which he recognizes and can understand, may be several times as large.

A child's "remarkable creative use of language" is seen in three-year-old Jonathan's discovery of night beauty as reported by Dr. Strang:

> "Right out of my bed
> I saw the yellow, shining moon
> The yellow shining moon—
> Was there a firefly?
> Yes—in the dark shining—
> I can see fireflies
> Right out of my bed.
> Fireflies and stars
> In the dark shining."[6]

Language, capacity to communicate, is at the basis of a child's relationship with others and his later success in school and life. The size and character of a child's vocabulary will depend on his native intelligence and the stimulus to learn and speak which he has from his environment. If there are no books, no interesting things with which to play, no children in the home; if his parents never talk to each other or to him, or have only a meager vocabulary, how will he learn to talk well? Children have stopped talking when they have been compared unfavorably with another child who is quite loquacious, or have developed in some other way an emotional block.

One of our leading educators has said that if a child's questions are answered intelligently and wisely, by the time he is six and starts to school he will know half of all he will ever know.

## He Becomes a Person

We talk about personality a great deal, but hardly know what it is. A helpful definition is given in *Personality in the Making*, the fact-finding report of the Mid-century White House Conference on Children and Youth: "We mean by personality the thinking, feeling, acting human being, who, for the most part, conceives of himself as an individual separate from other individuals and objects. This human being does not *have* a personality; he *is* a personality."[7]

At first he cannot distinguish his body from persons or things. He does not know where he begins or where he ends. As Lindgren says, "His mother's breast is as much a part of him as his own fist, which also finds its way into his mouth."[8]

As I was watching a fifteen-months-old boy who was sitting on the floor, he toppled over and bumped his head. He righted himself and with a puzzled look felt his head with both hands. Then he leaned over and bumped his head again and again, trying to see what it was that got bumped, what his head was like and what relation it bore to him. Only little by little does he come to know that his body is separate from other objects, with all of its parts connected and vitally related.

In the same slow way, through his interaction with other persons, he becomes aware of himself as a person. Or, as Erickson would say, he achieves a sense of autonomy. A pup will become a dog without any association with other puppies or dogs, but a baby will never become a person in the full sense of that word except through fellowship with persons. His sense of being a self develops as he moves on toward his second year. It is necessary, if he is going to be an independent human being, for him to assert himself against us. A mother whose little boy was not quite two years old said to me, "For weeks if I tell Bill not to put something in his mouth he'll put it in his eye, against his nose, his cheek, and slide it just as near his mouth as possible without putting it in, watching me all the time out of the corner of his eye." One day he may put it in. He almost has to for the development of his sense of being a person in his own right.

I saw this sense of selfhood flicker into being as I was sitting on the floor turning the pages of a magazine with a child twenty-two-and-a-half months old. We came to a big picture of a baby. He looked at it, patted it, saying, "Baybee, Baybee." Then straightening up, and putting his hand on his chest, he cried almost ecstatically, "Baybee! Baybee!" "Yes," I said, "you are a baby," and he smiled with delight. It may have been only his response to the approval in my tone.

His sense of being a person is not very clear and his hold on his own identity is not very strong. In one family a boy not quite three was promoted from a crib-like affair into a room and bed which his older brother Tommy had vacated. The next morning his father went in and said, "Good morning, Tommy!" Immediately came the protest, "I'm not Tommy, I'm Sammy." "Oh, no, you're Tommy. This is Tommy's room, this is Tommy's bed, you are certainly Tommy." There was a look of bewilderment in the little fellow's eyes, as he said rather pitifully, "I'm Sammy; see my nightie." He was the only one of the children who wore canton flannel night-clothes. His only way of convincing himself that he was himself—and, he felt, of convincing his father—was by gripping the sleeve of his little pajama top. A child may ask, "Why am I Johnny and not Billy? Why am I not a tree?" Another may pray, "God bless me. You know my name, I'm Danny," a bit unsure just who he is.

Not only does his sense of being a person develop out of his relationship with other persons; but the kind of person he judges himself to be will depend on the kind of persons he is with and the way in which they feel about him and treat him. The first three years of a child's life are acutely important for his development as a person.

Imagine a child who has just learned to walk, rejoicing in his achievement yet somewhat uncertain of himself, coming to a doorsill between two rooms.⁹ Can he make it? Dare he try? He and his mother see each other at the same time. She may say and do any one of a number of things.

She may rush to him, crying, "Wait for mother, don't try that by yourself," then pick him up and lift him over. After that he may think, "I can't really do anything by myself. When things get hard I'd better turn to mother for help. If she won't help me, all is lost. I don't reckon I'll ever grow up and be able to go it alone."

She may look at him with cold, hard eyes, in complete indifference. He may say to himself, "Mother doesn't care whether I do it or not. She doesn't care for me. Nobody does. Well, I'll have to do it by myself, I'll go it alone, now and always. I don't care for her, or people either. I'll have to be hard too."

She may say as he hesitates, "Aren't you ashamed of yourself, a great big boy and afraid to step over that low sill? Billy could do it when he was your age." His reaction may be, "She's right, I am afraid. I am not as capable as my brother, I'm really no good. Life is too big for me, I'll never get anywhere."

She may smile encouragingly or offer a finger, or say, "Of course you can, try it!" Emboldened by her attitude, he may say to himself, "Of course I can. Mother loves me, people are friendly and helpful. I shall be like that. Life is going to be a joyous, co-operative experience."

Now suppose mother again and again in many situations assumes one of these attitudes, and others in the home behave in the same way toward this boy growing into selfhood. Can he judge or esteem himself, except on the basis of his experience with the people closest to him? Dr. Cooley spoke long ago of the "looking-glass self," the reflection we see of ourselves as we look at the reaction of others toward us. A child can't help generalizing from his daily experiences, drawing conclusions about himself, building his own "self-image." "I am a person who can do things," he says deep down inside, "whom people like." Or, "I'm a person who is afraid of people, they don't like me, I'll never amount to much." Or, "I have to be hard and I'll be hard; people better get out of my way."

This is somewhat exaggerated, and oversimplified, for personality is very complex and a child's relationships are subtle and many. Yet there is enough in what I have said to cause mother and father to think seriously, and ask themselves several questions:

"Will he ever grow up, learn to think and act as an independent person, if I never let him face and solve difficult problems? If I help him before he needs or asks for help?

"Do I really love him with an unselfish love which puts his welfare first and frees him to be his own best self? Or, am I holding him close because I have no one else who will respond to my affection, and I am meeting my need through him? Do I condemn him, sharply contrast him with others, not that he might become a better boy, but because my pride suffers if he is not superior?

"Do I, because of my failure to understand and respect his rate of growth, demand more of him than at his age he can do, and so discourage him and make him feel guilty? Or, do I insist that he do much less, and so encourage him to be content with mediocrity?

"Out of his interaction with persons and situations, is he developing a sense of achievement, satisfaction, trust, courage, friendliness, love? Or, is there a growing feeling of frustration, fear, guilt, hostility?"

The self-concept (the way he thinks of himself) he builds during these early years through our attitude toward him and the way in which we deal with him, will be difficult for him to change in later life. Sometimes one experience goes deep. Usually it is the cumulative effect of his relation with people, their attitude toward him day after day, which will determine the way he thinks of himself.

Over a period of many years I have asked hundreds of students to describe their earliest memory and whether or not the experience they recalled had affected their later life. The memories are of all kinds—pleasant and unpleasant. Practically all of the students could recall events before six, most of them happenings at three or four. They remember an amazing variety of things—falls, into a creek, from a chair, into the mud, down the stairs, over a pew; cuts, burns, births, deaths, birthdays, Christmases, trips, moving into beautiful new homes; parents playing with them, taking them to interesting places, loving them; parents quarreling with each other, ignoring them, punishing them unjustly and severely, without the love or the expression of it for which they longed, playing favorites —the list would fill a book.

No one could read these papers year after year and not see in childhood experiences the roots of happiness, love, a secure, confident attitude toward life; or a feeling of insecurity, inadequacy, even hostility.

Here is a paper typical of many:

"I was dressed in a new *white dimity* with a *pink ribbon* in my hair. Grandmother had taken particular pains with the pink ribbon. This was the day my little brother was to come home from the hospital and I was dressed in honor of the occasion. I was beginning to get tired of waiting so patiently when the front door opened. Mother came in first and then Father with the blue and white bundle in his arms. Grandmother stepped forward to take the baby. Father took Mother's arm to lead her up the steps. Everybody talked at once.

" 'Is the baby's bed ready?'

" 'Yes, all ready. Would you like something to eat? A glass of milk?'

" 'No, thank you. It is nearly time for supper.'

" 'Terrible weather! Hope he doesn't take cold. Oh, dear, put him to bed. He'll go right to sleep.'

"I crept back against the wall until they all went upstairs. I was only three, so I could not quite understand. Big tears rolled slowly down my cheeks. *Not even Mother* had seen the pink ribbon in my hair."

Even today that girl is jealous of her brother, and feels inferior when he is present, sure he will be noticed and she passed by. We know, of course, that this experience was related to her whole life in the home.

So many experiences are buried deep, and while they may not be brought back to consciousness they profoundly affect life. Psychoanalytical studies are full of case histories that reveal this. It has become common knowledge. One of Loretta Young's television programs was built around a wife who went to pieces in an elevator, and couldn't, despite the strong exercise of her will, stand being in a small, closed place. Back of it was an experience with a father who unjustly accused her of breaking a plate and shut her in a closet, trying to make her confess her sins of carelessness and lying, of which she was innocent, creating in her a terrible feeling of hostility and of guilt because she hated him. She had forgotten it, the self had to put it aside for its own protection, but the emotional charge remained to make her life terribly unhappy.

Voices have been raised to warn us about putting too much emphasis on these years, saying that we haven't sufficient scientific proof that they are as important as some claim. Parents are urged not to get so anxious about their own relationship to their preschool children that they will create an atmosphere of tension which will be hurtful; not to feel hopeless if all does not go well in the home during this period, nor to think when it has come to an end that their duty has been done, that they can take it easy now for the child's life is inalterably set in the right direction.

Dr. Bossard, professor of sociology at the University of Pennsylvania, makes this clear in his excellent book, *Parent and Child*. He assures us that life is plastic to the end, that the family's influence is felt through all the succeeding years, that each new group affects life, that later education and training have high value. "The individual is the result of what adolescence, youth, and adulthood do to childhood experiences."[10] He would say to parents, "Do not despair. Do not rest on your oars."

Yet with Dr. Bossard's caution in mind, one might do well to meditate on Dr. Gesell's statement: "It may be doubted whether all of his scholastic strides taken together bulk for as much as his brilliant advance from the stage of protoplasmic vegetation at birth to the mastery of physical and personal relations—language, art, and science—which he has attained when he first slings his school bag over his shoulder. . . . Though he may not learn to read in the preschool years, he is mastering the alphabet of life."[11]

There is a Chinese proverb, "No matter how the twig is bent, 'twill straighten as a tree"; but it would be better to hold in mind one from the West, "As the twig is bent, the tree's inclined."

These last weeks, just outside my study window, a robin built her nest and raised her brood. The fledglings were so little, so naked, so helpless. But mother robin knew exactly what to do, and cared for them so expertly that in what seemed to me an incredibly short time the nestlings were ready one by one to try out their wings, and were gone. How simple life would become for human parents, if by heredity they were equipped as well for rearing their young! Perhaps, too simple!

While we are prepared by our biological inheritance to create life, it does not give us the knowledge, or the skills, or the love to guide that life to its fulfillment. It is only through thoughtful observation and honest study that we can acquire some understanding of the way in which a child grows, the drives that lie behind his behavior, and the helpful methods that have been devised for his upbringing.

But knowledge of child psychology, mastery of the latest techniques for training Sammy, or Sally, are not enough, if there is not in our home joy and love—love of parents for each other and for their child. It may be better to leave books alone, or pass up lectures, if they will create in us such fears or guilt feelings that we shall become tense and unhappy or make us try to bring up our son, or daughter, in strict conformity with a set of rules, forgetful that he is an individual who differs from all other boys and girls.

It is better not to have a child unless we want him, plan for him, and will give him not only care, but love—the unconditioned, free, forgiving love which our Father has given us, the love that "never faileth." The love he needs will be ours, and will grow, only as we remember and follow the laws of friendship.

# Love During School Days

*I*T WAS JAMES RUSSELL LOWELL, I think, who said, "The child loudens into a boy." He seems to do just that. He is not so lovable as the little fellow who is no more, nor so exciting as the teen-ager who is on the way. So he may not get the attention he needs. This in-between period has been referred to as the "forgotten years."

## He Goes to School

School is for him a great adventure, especially if he hasn't been to nursery school or kindergarten, and there are no older brothers or sisters who, having blazed the trail for him, can assure him that life in school is good, and give him a helping hand. Some children take to it happily as a duck to water, others are hesitant or afraid. One jerks her hand out of mother's and joyously runs away to join the children; another turns, hides her face in mother's dress, and begins to cry. Mother, because her own pride is involved, may shake her, slap her, threaten her, say sharply, "Aren't you ashamed to act like this? Look at that other little girl, she doesn't hang on to her mother." With the only result that the little body is shaken with more violent sobs, and the hands clutch more appealingly.

If mother could have realized that fear of the unknown is one of our chief fears, and fear of people is high on the list; if she had just taken time and thought to prepare Sally for the big step into this threatening new world—all might have been different.

## Prepare Him for School

Angelo Patri, who out of his years of service in the public schools of New York writes so sagely, in his *Home and School* has a chapter captioned "The First Day at School," in which he urges teachers and parents to prepare the child for that awesome first day. For the effect of his initial experiences, good or ill, may influence his whole later attitude toward school and learning. Take him to the school before the opening day, show him through the building, be sure he knows the location of the toilets, let him drink at all the fountains, swing on all the swings in the playground. Spend a little time in his room, introduce him to his teacher; hope that she smiles, for if she does all may be well.

Now that you have made a good contact with the school keep in touch with it. Join the PTA, and try to see that parents and teachers think and talk through their problems together. Don't criticize the school except on the basis of fact. Your child may not be an accurate reporter. If something is really wrong, wouldn't it be better to discuss it with teacher or principal, rather than to condemn the school to your child or friends? Dr. Rudolph Flesch's racy book, *Why Johnny Can't Read*, which contrasts the new "look-say" method with the old phonetic method, has created much excitement in Richmond. Such a question would be just the kind to be considered objectively by parents and teachers.

If Sammy, after a good start, suddenly doesn't want to go to school, find out why. It may be he is being pushed around by a bigger boy, or has been laughed at because of the funny way he talks, or can't do an assigned task, or fears to leave home because something may happen to you; Johnny's mother fell down the stairs and was carried to the hospital while he was away at school. Always before we know what to do about a child's behavior, there is the question, *why?* to be faced and answered.

But a child really can't be prepared for that first day at school by a few hours spent in surveying the school prior to its opening in the fall. Can we suddenly demand that he be a "big boy," comfortable in a completely new situation, happy away from his mother, when we have kept him at home, made him dependent on us, encouraged him up to now in his baby ways? Go back in your thinking to the story of the doorsill. Ask yourself, "What kind of a self-image have I helped him build? Has he had friends of his own age to play with?" I know people who have been largely influenced in buying a home by the fact that there were children in the neighborhood who matched their children in age.

Have we let him help us in the work of the home? He is so eager to do it. But it takes less time and effort to do everything ourselves and to "shoo" him off into a corner with his toys, or turn him loose in the yard if it is fenced in. Yet how can he grow unless he learns to share experiences with us, to do things that are helpful? Those first days at school may spotlight our failure during the years that preceded them. That he can't adjust easily to new surroundings and people, and assume responsibilities that should now be his, may not be his fault but ours. Each new period of life builds on and is conditioned by the years that have gone before.

## Grant Him More Freedom

Try to keep from thinking of him as a little child who must be constantly guided and protected. Drop the word "child" out of your vocabulary after he reaches the fourth grade, or before. Think of him as a boy, refer to him as one. There are mothers who take their boys and girls to school and go for them, even drive their sons to a Scout meeting and wait for them. They are afraid for them to ride their bicycles, or go with their friends.

Much of our trouble at camp was with mothers. One mother in Texas phoned her son twice every week; not just to learn what he was doing and to give him news of the family, but to make him homesick and encourage him to demand that she come for him and take him back to Texas. We had a homesick boy or two every summer, but we had more trouble with lonely mothers who haunted camp, trailed around after their sons, were happy if they could make them unhappy and find an excuse to take them home. We wondered about their relationship to their husbands, the emptiness of their lives, the chance their sons had to grow up. Because the children are away from home more, and life may seem more full of danger for them, parents may be less democratic in their relationship with their boys and girls now that they are older than when they were younger. If we encourage them to make choices, to assume responsibility as their ability increases, if we give them reasonable freedom now, they will be less apt to break over and demand unreasonable freedom later on.

## Encourage Him to Be Himself

It may be that before he was born we dreamed of the child we wanted to have, and walked with him in imagination through the years of his unfolding. We wanted him to be like we remembered ourselves to have been when we were small, or wanted to see our unrealized hopes fulfilled in him. We weren't smart, or popular, or athletic, or musical; so we nag, or push, or pull him that we may find in him what we missed, all the while not thinking of him, but of ourselves.

Perhaps we compare him with a younger or older brother or sister. "Why can't you be like Mary, or Bobby? They never give me any trouble, they are at the top of their class in school." With the result that jealousy burns in him toward brother or sister, resentment toward us, and he may become so discouraged and filled with bitterness that he falls below his own possibilities, or he may become rebellious and something of a problem child.

If we could just discover what are his particular gifts, be happy over them, help him develop them, praise him for what he can do and not condemn him because of what is beyond him, joy would fill his heart and we would have a new boy in the home and at school.

## Rejoice in His Growth

He may be harder to live with than when he was that dear little fellow, but life is for growth. How tragic it would be if his growth were arrested at six. *His body grows.* How sturdy he is, how strong, how active, how tireless, how well-co-ordinated. How hard he plays!

Whatever may be our theory of play, we know that play is the very life of our boys and girls. We should have done well if in the years before they started to school we had filled our back yards with every enticement to play—swings, sliding boards, ladders, sand piles, and such inexpensive things as old barrels and boxes, worn-out pots and pans, bricks and cardboard cartons. With children's ingenuity almost anything can be of value. We must be sure that there is a place where they can dig without endangering mother's flowers. Somewhere in this age boys seem to want to make an excavation that will lead them right down to China!

At nine the boy probably has a wider range of play activities than at any other time. He will still play in the back yard, roam the neighborhood on his bicycle or skates, engage in all sorts of informal games, while at the same time he is beginning to be interested in games that require skill. A year or two more and he will be somewhat ready for team games; though things go better if a coach is on hand, as too many may wish to pitch or bat at the same time.

Anyone who has worked with boys realizes how intensely concerned some of them are in developing skills in various sports. A youngster ten or eleven will practice endlessly his crawl stroke, or jack-knife dive. He will shoot baskets in the gym by the hour, and almost forget lunch as he seeks to improve his golf swing, or tennis backhand. It will be of great value to a boy or girl if, before he moves into his teens, he has mastered some athletic skills.

Often a boy who is in that self-conscious, awkward period won't play tennis or golf, or swim, because he doesn't want to be laughed at by smaller boys, as he appears a "dub" at what they do expertly. Several studies show that popularity in the teens is closely related to strength and athletic skills. The teenager must, therefore, play some games well if he is to gain standing in his group and develop self-confidence. Play—especially team games—has many values. Someone has said, "What you do to make a boy active you do to make him safe." Another has put it more positively, "What you do to make a boy active you do to make him good." Hard play releases aggressive tendencies in a regulated, socially accepted way, teaches self-control, fairness, courage, quick thinking, and co-operation. Here is father's chance to play with his boys, and to see that they are taught the skills they need to learn and the ideals of sportsmanship that should go with them.

We have put too much emphasis on sports in America and

should try to further other types of recreation—working with tools, nature study, photography, painting, music, and dramatics. Boys and girls are interested in making collections of all kinds, a boy's pockets or a drawer in a girl's room make this quite evident. This early interest can be capitalized for a valuable hobby that will last through life. Teach the youngsters to collect flowers, leaves, shells, butterflies, stamps, coins, good records, and their joy in them may never end.

## The Mind Grows

The foundation for the mind's growth is largely laid and its direction set in the preschool days. Now there is the new stimulus of teachers, and studies, and trips, and friends. The child's world widens and heightens until he has circled the globe and touched the stars.

We used to refer to the years nine to twelve as "the golden memory period." The term has been laid aside, as we know that memory is "a sticky interest" and that in later years he can recall what he wants to learn just as well as in the fourth, fifth, and sixth grades.

He has the memory of an elephant for the things that strike his interest. Make him a promise to take him fishing, or to a ball game, and he never forgets. At first I was chagrined at the way the boys at camp would pick up any inaccurate statement I made in referring to something in the world of sports. I might say, "Jesse Owens' Olympic record in the broad jump was 26′ 4″." A lad would stop me afterward, "No, Doctor, he jumped 26′, 5-5/16″." Or, "Ty Cobb led the American League in batting 10 times." "No, Doctor, he led it 12 times, 9 times in succession. His lifetime batting average was 367." Later I bought Menke's *Encyclopedia of Sports*, and tried to verify my facts before I spoke.

Imaginative play goes on for a year or two after the school doors open. Boys and girls constantly engage in make-believe play. Boys are cowboys, space men, Davy Crockett, or whatever the television programs, movies, or cereal boxes make the vogue. Girls play house, school, mother and child; and boys would too if our culture encouraged them. Imaginary companions take their departure when school days begin or shortly thereafter, unless an abnormal need keeps them alive.

We speak of the faith of a little child. He is credulous. His vivid imagination, his capacity to take fragments of different ideas and things and put them together into strange patterns, his lack of experience, his limited knowledge, and his trustfulness prepare him to believe anything. Santa Claus, fairies, myths, add zest and color to his daily life. But as year follows year his world becomes more realistic. He can think better now, and he has more facts from which he can draw his conclusions. An eleven-year-old girl was asked if she liked to read fairy stories. She replied with a sniff, "I like to read them to children."

At this time a boy may begin to wonder about the Bible stories he has been told. Not a few parents have been startled when a seven- or eight-year-old has abruptly asked, "Did God really make the world? How do you know?" "Are all the stories in the Bible true, every one of them?"

The Kindergarten period has been referred to as "The Age of Questions," and the Primary period as "The Age of the Vanishing Question." It may be that he stops asking questions because he is beginning to realize how little we know, or because we have shut him up. This we must not do, for it is through his questions that he learns. Kipling is not far from right, when he says,

> "I keep six honest serving-men
> (They taught me all I knew);

Their names are What and Why and When
And How and Where and Who."[1]

Education has been defined as "The art of preserving the curiosity of a child." Despite our efforts to silence him, unless they have been very severe he still has a driving curiosity. If he doesn't ask questions, it is not because he doesn't desire to know, but because many of them have been answered, and he now knows where to look for the answers, for he can read. Compton's Encyclopedia, or Britannica Junior, or the World Book ought to be right at hand. If our budget won't allow us to get one of these, many attractive books can be found at the ten cent store.

Probably reading is at its peak in the Junior period. Boys and girls read to get knowledge, or because they see others reading, or because life is boring and they want excitement, or because they are unhappy and want escape, or because they are lazy and it is one of the less taxing ways to amuse themselves.

If they don't read it may be because their parents don't read, or haven't read to them, and there are no books in the home; or because they have never learned to read well enough to enjoy a book, or haven't happened upon the kind of book that will set fire to their minds. Failure to be able to read well means that they are shut off from the world of books—history, biography, literature, science—and that they will stumble through high school and college, if they ever finish either. Being retarded in school, or dropping out, will result in unhappiness and may be one of the causes of delinquency.

There are those who defend the so-called comic books because they stimulate the interest of some children in reading, intrigue others to read faster and better. What a reflection upon the reading habits of our country that a billion copies are published every year, at a cost to the public of $100,000,000! It is not only boys and girls in the fourth, fifth, and sixth grades who are guilty. Comic books are read by those who are younger and much older. Traveling on trains and buses reveals that adults, chronologically speaking, are addicts too. While the art is bad, and the style poor, comics arrest the eye, they are packed with action, and for a dime a boy can make his own choice.

Like everything else, comics vary in value. The Committee on Evaluation of Comic Books, P. O. Box 1486, Cincinnati, which each year evaluates several hundred of these books, puts them in three classes—"no objection," "some objection," "objectionable." They run from *Classics Illustrated* and *Mickey Mouse,* to the *Vault of Horror* and the *Web of Evil.*

It is difficult to be sure just what their effect is on our youngsters, as *they* differ, and the *comics* differ. Some juvenile court judges say they cannot trace crime to comics, others believe that comics not only teach how to steal and murder, but arouse the desire to do evil. There are psychiatrists who claim that comics actually prevent crime by releasing aggressive feelings, hate, jealousy, guilt; that it is only those who are already maladjusted to whom comics make a hurtful appeal. On the other hand some of their colleagues contend that comics produce fears, intensify the feeling of hostility, break down moral ideals, and promote crime. While the book is probably one-sided, *Seduction of the Innocent,* by Dr. Frederic Wertham, shows clearly that some boys and girls are terribly hurt by some comic books.

What can we do about it? One determined mother associating with herself convinced persons and groups, as in Falls Church, Virginia, can change the type of comics put on the newsstands! We can help our youngsters choose the better comics by talking over the whole question with them, and developing some criteria by which to judge them. We can create an appetite for better reading by providing books that not only have value but are attractive in format and interesting in content.

One librarian stepped up the quality of the reading of her boys and girls by putting in the back of a book, "If you found this interesting you would like _____," then giving the title of a book on a little higher level. Above all we can try to give our youngsters such a rich, interesting life in the home, school, community, and church that unwholesome comics will lose their interest and be outgrown.

What of the other mass media of communication—movies, radio, television? They have potentially high value but, like the comics, vary widely. The same general suggestions made for helping Mary and Billy with comics would apply to them.

## The Junior Is Tough

The boy from nine to eleven is, as we have seen, robust in body. Strength is his, and exuberant energy. He is tough in attitude. He has a new sense of being a person, a new desire for status. He develops a new resistance to our demands. The spirit of adventure and recklessness throbs in him. While he can take care of himself better now, the accident rate in this period is very high. He pushes and wrestles and fights. We might think of him as saying,

> "Count that day lost whose low descending sun
> Sees no battle fought and won."

A coward is his supreme abomination. Rather than be called a "sissy" he would risk his life. When he is a bit older it is "chicken" from which he shrinks.

## *The Junior Goes with a Gang*

He wants an assured place in the group, or gang, of hard-running boys of his own age. He is aware of girls, and of what they think of him. But he doesn't want to play with them now, and even scorns them. His is a man's world whose approval he must have, to whose demands he must conform. He wants to wear what they wear, talk like them, do what they do. The gang may have secret grips, passwords, initiations; but often it is loosely organized about one or two able leaders. Its morality is usually below that of the individual members. It depends largely on the ideas and force of the boy who takes the lead. A suggestion is made and eight or ten boys race through the cabins at camp, dumping beds and making them into a shambles; at home they might throw rocks at the street lights. A constructive idea strikes them and they work hard in a hot sun to improve the tennis courts or golf course. What a need there is for Cub Scouts, boys' choirs, 4-H Clubs, and for attractive men to lead them. For the boy is a hero-worshiper.

Out of the give-and-take of life with his peers he comes to understand the kind of behavior the group will approve, and so learns to control himself, to get along with others. He learns, too, to enjoy life apart from his parents.

You have to know how to shift mental and emotional gears if you are asked to teach Juniors instead of the Kindergarten group with whom you have worked exclusively. Miss Elizabeth Shields, who for so many years was the wise director of the Children's Division of the Church School for the Presbyterian Church in the U. S., used to enjoy telling the story of a teacher of five-year-olds—those beribboned little girls, those darling little boys—who substituted one Sunday for a friend who taught a class of Junior boys. The lesson was on the

Exile, and she told the story with dramatic power. Then she asked, "What would you do if an old king would take you out of your nice home and carry you to a far land?" A boy said gruffly, "I'd get my knife and cut his guts out." It took the sensitive teacher days to recover!

Slang, "cuss-words," "sexy words"—"shockers," they are called—tumble out unexpectedly. They are a part of the gang vocabulary, and of his advancing years. He wants to appear grown-up. If we refuse to be shocked, indicate that adults know these words and many others, but do not think them appropriate to grown-up life or in a cultured home—and we have that kind of a home—the first time they are used may be the last time. Or, there may be no first time in not a "stuffy" home, but one in which ideals of speech and conduct have developed out of real companionship.

But there is another side to this lad. I have seen a boy at camp indignantly throw off his mother's arm when she put it around his shoulders, and draw back in apparent disgust when she tried to kiss him. Later, I have noticed that same boy walking through camp swinging his mother's arm as he held her hand, and have seen him snuggled up to her, enjoying her arm about him, as they sat in the front seat of the family car.

## He Wants a Pal

The boy hungers for a friend—a chum. It was my function for years to try to help the very homesick boys. I would walk with them through camp, interpret its activities, introduce them to the coaches and men in charge of arts and crafts, tell them stories, read to them, play with them, even help them build water wheels in the stream flowing into the lake—something forbidden to others—all to no avail. Then suddenly a boy would meet another boy and something would click between them—just why I never fully knew—and away they'd go together, jabbering at a great rate. For days they'd be inseparable, then he might find another boy congenial. The best cure for homesickness, I discovered as I worked with many an unhappy boy, was for him to find a friend. With older boys the pairing off might last the whole summer. Don't let us be too concerned if a ten-year-older picks up a friend of whom we do not fully approve. He may need him then. If the new boy is not really congenial, the friendship probably will not last long.

## He May Be Aggressive

A certain amount of aggressiveness is necessary and wholesome. It drives a boy to face difficult tasks, to overcome obstacles, to venture into a none-too-friendly world, to throw off the yoke of the home, to fight for his own proper rights and the rights of others, to stand solidly on his own two feet.

But here and there you will find a boy with an overdose. He bullies smaller boys, or weaker boys, or boys who won't fight back. The trouble is within himself. Just what it is we may not be sure. He probably feels insecure, inferior, and must shove someone else around to build his own ego, to be able to maintain his self-respect, to live with himself. Possibly he failed at school, or didn't rate in his group, or was beaten in game after game, or has begun to doubt the love of his mother as she gives more and more time to his younger brother who is sick. It may be there is a deep-lying hostility in his heart toward a teacher, or his parents. One of the helpful discoveries of depth psychology is the existence in us of ambivalent feelings. We may both love and hate the same person, and at the same time. Look at it on the simplest level. A mother gives her baby a bottle, he loves her. She thinks he has had enough so she takes it away; but he is still hungry and feels anger toward her. She picks him up and cuddles him against her breast; he loves her. The phone rings and she abruptly puts him down. A gossipy friend keeps her a long time. He frets and cries and again anger builds up toward her. This process, often in more subtle ways, goes on all the time.

I have had a little child say to me, "I like you, I don't like you," until it became almost a chant. "You're a nice Mummie," a girl said to her mother, "but sometimes you're mean." There it is. We see this in ourselves if we are honest. We have ambivalent feelings toward our children, for sometimes they're "nice," and sometimes they're "mean." We shall think of ourselves later. Now let us look for a moment at this child. He doesn't know how to handle his hostility; it frightens him, or gives him a sense of guilt. In our culture children should love their parents. Yet at times he doesn't love, so guilt feelings develop. Most of this may be below his awareness, so he doesn't know what is the source of his guilt, or of the anxiety which accompanies it. It is all quite vague, but he is restless, unhappy, and he may vent his hostility on brothers and sisters, or teacher, or playmates through aggressive behavior. He may steal to revenge himself on his parents by shaming them, or to make them, or someone else, punish him to ease his sense of guilt. There may be, however, almost fifty-seven varieties of causes behind stealing.

How devastating all this can be to a child, if he is not sure of his mother's love. How healing it is to him if he is certain that her love is so deep and strong that she can accept him despite all his hostilities and sense of guilt. It may be relief will come if he is sure he can even say to his mother, "I hate you," and know it will be understood and forgiven, and the relationship maintained unbroken. Mother may help a little if, when he is terribly angry, she turns him loose on a punching bag, or lets him bang away with a hammer and nails. If he is old enough to build something of value, all the better.

It would help us in dealing with these youngsters if we could learn to ignore their behavior. A boy comes thundering into the house, and thunders out. We can make trouble for ourselves and him if we establish a rule that he must come in quietly. He likes to make a noise, it gives him a sense of power. He has been at school all day, sitting still for much of the time, under discipline the whole time. Now he is free and his pent-up energy must express itself, like the rush of a stream after the dam is broken. Do we want a boy or a mouse? We want him to behave in certain ways, and make demands upon him to conform. But are our rules for his development, or to save us trouble, or to secure the praise of our neighbors?

## *This Too Will Pass*

It would comfort us when we are on edge because of his strange behavior to remember that most of it is natural for boys of his age, and our son is like the boy next door. Talk to his mother; misery loves company, and is helped by knowing that others are afflicted in a similar way.

A word I picked up somewhere has made hard days easier— "This too will pass." Much of what we think of as problem behavior will be left behind as life climbs to a new stage. Only if it is excessive and prolonged need we begin to feel concern. We might keep in mind, however, Christabel Morley Cordell's jingle,

> "Knowing it's just a passing phase
> Consoles the harried mother
> Until she learns, as years go by,
> One phase succeeds another."[2]

One more suggestion—nothing gives him quite the sense of security, the assurance of your love, which is the very basis of his life, as for you to be at home when he gets back from school. He may just throw open the door, holler, hear your answer, drop his books, and race away. At home for that! It seems silly. But to know you are there, to catch the note of confidence and love in your voice as you call back, are a bit like the everlasting arms which undergird and lift. An empty house —a hollow echo—and a lonely, insecure little boy or girl may hang disconsolately about the yard, or go off to play, or get in trouble. "It makes me so mad," an eight-year-older grumbled, "when I come home and Mother is not there!"

Mothers who have really understood their children have known this all along. Now the psychiatrists in our guidance clinics are crying it aloud. Dr. Bossard, a sociologist, is emphatic: "It may be that the most important need of a school child under ten years of age is to have a mother awaiting his return home, and that the lack of this maternal presence is one of the most serious costs of the gainful employment of women with young children."[3] This is one of the questions to be thought through by father and mother before they agree it is best for her to go to work. Could the fact of working mothers have anything to do with the increase in juvenile delinquency? In 1953 almost 25% of all mothers with children under 18 were working; in 1940 only 10% were at work. Two million of the mothers working in 1953 had one or more children under six.

Billy Graham's mother said, "I made it a point to be at home always at the time my children reached home from school." Could that be one of the reasons, under God, why a man so young, comparatively unschooled, could have so much quiet self-confidence, as he speaks to tens of thousands, associates with world-renowned savants, dines with royalty?

# Love and Adolescence

*I*NFANCY with its helplessness, then school days with its first real venture from home; now the wheel of life turns again and our boys and girls are lifted to another level of existence—adolescence! Dr. Esther Richards in *Behaviour Aspects of Child Conduct* begins her chapter on Adolescence, "I am always rather amused at the interest which the word 'adolescence' attracts on any program. Like the delinquent, the defective, and the degenerate, the adolescent has come to be classified as an abnormality about which something should be done as soon as possible."[1] Yet adolescence only means to grow, to grow from childhood into maturity. There is nothing strange nor abnormal about that. It is natural, normal, inevitable—the period of transition during which the boy or girl becomes a man or woman, the bridge over which all must pass on the journey from childhood to adulthood. What makes it difficult for us as we try to understand teen-agers is that they shuttle back and forth across the bridge. One day they behave like little children, the next, they are gravely mature; on a third, they are in-between. It is very confusing.

Adolescence has been called "life's greatest definite, natural change," and much was said two decades ago of the "storm and stress" of this period. At the present we are putting more emphasis on the fact that it is continuous with childhood, as our youth are so largely what the preceding years have made them. Dr. Richards tells of a mother who brought her twelve-year-old son to her because of his irritability and temper tantrums, caused by "adolescence." As they were talking, the boy, who had been left in the waiting room, burst in without knocking, shouting, "I'm tired hanging around. I'm going out." The mother coaxed, then threatened, but Henry turned and ran down the stairs with his mother after him. She caught him and marched him back, saying, "He never would have done that two years ago." Dr. Richards surmised that it wouldn't have happened now if bad habit patterns had not been building through the years. "I know it's childish for me to cry and have temper tantrums," said a fourteen-year-old girl, "but that's the only way I could get what I needed in my family." It is not strange that this period has been called "the judgment time for parents."

We used to stress the coming of pubescence, the maturing of the glands and organs associated with sex, as the cause of adolescence. Now we recognize that involved in it are his whole growing body and maturing mind, and the expanding, changing, and increasingly complex environment in which members of the other sex play a primary role.

Adolescence might be thought of as a comparatively *new* period from the standpoint of the history of the race. Primitive peoples make no provision for ten or twelve years of an in-between life. Yesterday the boy was a child. Today he is initiated into the tribe, marries and takes his place with the men as they go out to hunt, or fish, or fight.

In 1956 we do not so quickly, or so evidently, say to him, "Now you are a man!" In my day a boy at least did put on long pants at a certain age; now he is given them as soon as he can walk.

In our country, in days not far behind us, adolescence as we know it now was only to be enjoyed by the sons of the rich. Some of the changes in our culture which we have already discussed, and others more recent, made this period what it is now, and created many of the problems associated with it. The shift of our population to the city, the increased use of machinery, and the enormous advance in the wealth of the nation make it unnecessary for everybody to work to support the family. With this came the feeling of parents that they did not wish their children to work so hard as they had done, and their desire for them to have a good education. All the states require boys and girls to attend school until they are sixteen, and several have raised the age limit to seventeen or eighteen.

In 1905 there were only 210,000 pupils in high school, while in 1952 there were 7,500,000 enrolled—85.9% of the boys and girls in that age range. In 1900 only 4% of our young people from 18 to 21 were in college, now 25% of this age group are enrolled.

Most of us hardly realize the way in which the First World War speeded up the social changes which were in the making, and brought into being what was known as "the mad decade," or "the decade of abnormalcy." Goodwin Watson in *Youth After Conflict* writes: "The American young people who reached adolescence shortly after the First World War were the most talked-about youth generation in human history. They were the Jazz Age, the Flappers, the Sheiks, and Flaming Youth. Earlier in American history the problems of youth were not distinguished from those of any other age group."[2] One of the tragedies of today is that young people have been lifted out of their proper setting, and put over against children and adults as almost wholly different from, and antagonistic to, these other groups. If we could realize that youth and adults are just people, each with his own hopes and fears, who need to work together if we are to meet successfully the issues that face our nation and our world!

The depression, World War II, the Korean War, and the

present world uncertainty have not made life easier for youth, nor for their parents. Our difficulty is increased by the way in which the authority of the Bible is being challenged, our moral ideals are being undermined by the conception of relativity, our standards of sex behavior set by what Dr. Kinsey finds the majority of people doing. Right and wrong are not so sharply defined now. Add all this together, and we must not think of young people *as* problems, but as those who, with us, *have* serious problems of many kinds.

Some such background will be of value as we try to live helpfully with the happy or troubled Billys and Marys who are in our homes.

We need not expect, if our youngster's life has been normal up to now, any tremendous emotional upheaval, any sudden turn for the worse brought on by adolescence. We can anticipate the future with confidence rather than fear, knowing that the days ahead will be interesting, even exciting, rather than terrible.

If they don't behave just as we think they should, perhaps we don't understand what is proper teen-age conduct. We should wait a bit before we judge, and then hesitate to blame as the boys and girls are in the grip of their past and in a difficult world. Blame usually is of little help anyway.

To blame ourselves doesn't help either; it increases our sense of guilt, makes us more tense, harder to live with. Life for us hasn't been easy. We have had to live in the same world. It may be that we have an opportunity, in this period when they are changing, to offset our failures of yesterday, to help them toward a better understanding of themselves and life.

Now we can look more definitely at Sally and Sammy to see what is happening to them and what their needs are.

## Their Bodies Grow

In the past, adolescence has been divided into three periods: early, 12 through 14; middle, 15 through 17; late, 18 through 23. More recently those in the last period have been referred to as young adults. We can't separate these stages sharply and say, "Now is the time to look for this to happen," or "Well, that's over and done with." Young people differ from each other and the periods shade into each other. You may say to Mary, "Act your age!" But you may not be quite sure what her age is, and neither may she be certain.

Yet as life goes on, there is a difference. One night at a rather amorous movie I was sitting between two boys, one thirteen, the other sixteen. When the couple kissed for the first time there was a heartfelt sigh from the sixteen-year-old and an exclamation of digust from the boy thirteen. Once more they embraced, the sigh deepened. "What, again!" came from my left. When her suitor really began to show his affection, "Ah-h-h," said the lad on my right; "that's the best part of the picture." It was almost more than the other could stand. "Gee," he exclaimed, "is the nut going to massage her whole face!" There is a difference between the periods!

Growth in height and weight is rapid during the first period and into the second. Boys may continue to grow slowly during the college years, reaching their maximum stature at about nineteen. Girls achieve their height during high school. Some grow with unbelievable speed. Larry Kelly, the famous Yale end of years ago, shot up six inches in his fourteenth year; Gary Cooper, thirteen inches in his fifteenth year. A mother told me that she had her son measured for a suit, but before the tailor could complete it, it was too small. This isn't easy for them or for us.

Girls start growing a year or two earlier than boys, and from eleven or twelve through thirteen or fourteen are taller and heavier. Some girls may feel superior, boys resentful. It is easy to see why boys and girls of this age don't mix well at parties. Cole says, "There is some basis for the popular observation that a girl of thirteen is already a young lady, while a lad of thirteen is still a little boy."[3]

Much of youth's difficulty is caused by this strange experience of rapid growth. For a girl to mature early and find herself towering over her classmates, or to enter this period late and have them look down upon her, is very embarrassing, and makes it hard for her to adjust to her group or to herself. She needs to be assured that after a bit most of these inequalities will be straightened out.

There is the girl who will be relatively quite tall, and the boy who will be very short. This creates problems for both, for our culture demands that girls be comparatively short, and boys tall and strong. To be different, is to feel strange and out of place. Is it surprising that that boy of yours who is called "runt" acts the clown, hopeful that he will get favorable attention from the group, or that your beanpole girl likes to stay at home so much? She may already begin to wonder if she will ever have a chance to get married. One of Walt Disney's artists felt so keenly the difficulty of the tall girl that he organized a "Tip-toppers' Club" to bring them in contact with boys who were taller.

Life may be miserable for the excessively fat boy or girl. Small boys trooped from one end of our camp to the other just to look at a fifteen-year-older who weighed two hundred forty pounds. For him it was like being in a circus. How necessary it is for parents of a boy like that to understand how he feels. To criticize, blame, laugh, may almost destroy him. He needs help in developing some talent that will give him standing in his group. He must know that mother and father are proud of him and love him.

Unfortunately the body doesn't grow evenly, and we speak of the awkwardness of this age. The boy is self-conscious because of the new emotions that he feels, and the new experiences he is facing. Students are not agreed on whether his self-consciousness causes awkwardness, or his gawkiness makes him self-conscious. Undoubtedly they are interactive. To send him from the table because he turns over a glass of milk won't help. He certainly didn't mean to do it. To laugh when she stumbles over her own feet, or crouches so her neck won't seem too long, will only add to her unhappiness. Help them to know that for them "this too will pass." Someone speaks of "a lanky boy whose bolts need tightening." Well, at sixteen they are tightened, and we have champions in several sports at that age. The girl at sixteen is all symmetry and grace.

We are aggravated by their enormous appetites, they eat so fast and are unfillable. I have heard of fathers who sent their sons from the table because their boys' plates came back for "seconds" before they had a chance to serve themselves. It would have helped them if they had known that a study of boys between 13 and 16 at a prep school showed that they needed more calories than a laboring man requires. A girl, when she is growing fastest, needs as many as an active woman. We used to be cautioned against letting them eat between meals, today we are advised that they may need food then. If their appetite is all out of reason we may begin to ask the question why. Fat boys or girls may be omnivorous because they get some satisfaction from food when their hunger for the approval of their group is denied.

We are annoyed because they often seem so lazy. One mother complained that her daughter just wants to sit, doesn't wish to go out to play, or to go to camp, says she's "tired"! Another mother, whose boy when asked to run an errand for her claimed that he was so tired, told him to go when he was rested. "But, Mother!" he protested, "I'm tired all the time." Much of their energy is consumed in growing, and they may play so hard that they are exhausted when they get home.

On the other hand we may be disturbed by their exuberant energy, their display of strength. Measured by certain tests, a boy at eleven is twice as strong as he was at six, and at sixteen twice as strong as he was at eleven. The realization of his own strength, this new sense of power, is partly responsible for his growing feeling of independence.

## They Grow in Their Capacity to Think

There is no new birth of mental powers at this time. Reason doesn't erupt like a wisdom tooth. It has been steadily growing through the years, as his knowledge has increased, his horizons widened through reading, travel, meeting different people, and his capacity to put facts side by side and draw his own conclusions has developed through experience. Just as his body has been growing, so has his capacity to think grown. There has been considerable discussion about just when he becomes mature intellectually, or to put it somewhat differently, when his mental powers stop growing. Scholars today are encouraging those of us who are older by putting the age later and later. Our concern now is that mental growth is very rapid in early adolescence and continues through a youth's later years. This means that, while he may not have quite the judgment that only long experience and broad knowledge can give, he can now really think. In the early years of this period

44601

he is interested in the concrete, everyday experiences of life, facts of all kinds. As the years go on he can think in abstract terms, is at home in the realm of ideas, is concerned about meanings, tries to work out for himself a system of values, a satisfying philosophy of life.

His capacity to think and the way he thinks will depend upon the equipment with which he began life, and the stimulus that has been given him through the books he has read, the situations in which he has been placed, and the people—parents, teachers, friends, and acquaintances—whom he has known.

We who are his parents must recognize his capacity to think, and the fact that while he may not have organized his knowledge fully and it may be spotty and unbalanced, he knows a lot, and what is in his mind may not go on all fours with what is in ours. If the gap in years between us is wide, he has studied different texts in high school and college, and been taught by different methods than those used in our day.

Some of our children may be smarter than we are—genius has a way of skipping over a generation—and may actually know more in several fields. Many youngsters almost pull their hair out in exasperation as our attitude toward them forces them to say, "Mother and Daddy don't believe we can think, don't give us credit for knowing anything. They tell us what is what, and that's the end. They never listen to us, give us a chance to say what's on our minds." If we would just listen we might learn much, and our willingness to listen might put our fellowship on a better basis.

We and they are often bound by the relation we have maintained with them through the preceding years. Have we dictated or discussed, listened or laid down the law, taken them by the hand when the road forked, or only guided them so they might find the way for themselves? Can we change our attitude now? Do we really want to? Again it may be a matter of pride. If we feel somewhat insecure we may be unwilling to expose our ignorance, so we won't discuss. How much more wholesome the atmosphere would be if Daddy or Mother could be free to say to son or daughter, "You are right, I was wrong about that." They know it anyhow. It would give them a new confidence in themselves—and in us— if we could just be honest.

It is possible that we are brilliant and our children aren't, that we know much more than they do. Will it help them if we make them conscious of their ignorance, or if we insist that they get high grades because we did? The competition— I dislike the word, and the conditions that lie behind it—becomes keener and keener as boys and girls move from grade school to junior high, to high, and to college. In the institutions which draw their students from wider areas they are thrown with abler boys and girls in increasing numbers. We judge ability by comparison. Dr. George Preston, for many years the Commissioner of Mental Hygiene for the State of Maryland, says, "I once lived in an institution for mental defectives, and as long as I stayed *inside* the institution I was an outstanding genius."[4] Your boy might have been close to the top of his class at grade school, but at high school and college he just struggles along in the valley. Don't press him to do more than he can do, or blame him if he fails. Tests of high school students show that fear of failure at school, and of what parents will say or do about the failure, haunts many boys and girls. While we desire our children to measure up to their best possibilities, and grow through the self-discipline that exacting study requires, for them to accept an impossible goal can only result in strain, unhappiness, failure, and a sense of guilt. We may drive Sammy because we wish the credit of having a successful son. What a lift it is to our egos to be able to say, so casually, to a friend, "We've just heard that our daughter has been elected to Phi Beta Kappa."

She may not be doing well in high school because she is physically under par, or because she belongs to too many organizations and goes to too many meetings. "Busyness," dashing here and there, being able to boast of how much one has to do, seem a part of "rating." Perhaps the boy with whom she has been going steady has found that new girl attractive, or she and Mary, her best friend, have had a misunderstanding, or the teacher on whom she had a crush has seemed to ignore her. A tangle in interpersonal relationships can make school work appear of small importance, or even despite a determined purpose may make study impossible. Their minds just refuse to work. If our son or daughter is falling below his known capacity, we have to help him find, and work through, the cause. Once more we face the ever-recurring and tormenting question, *Why?*

Sometimes there just seems to be a slump year in school which has to be waited out. A brilliant young doctor who had led his class at Medical College told me he hardly knew where he was during his sophomore year at high school and wondered how he had passed. He was so busy growing physically and emotionally, life had become so complex, that his mind wouldn't function. About all parents can do at a time like that is to be understanding and patient, and if they can find the smallest thing that son or daughter has done well, to express appreciation.

If he comes to us with a question about his work or life, let us answer it as thoughtfully as if an adult faces us. We might, as some doctors do, postpone trying to help him until we have consulted our books, or a wise friend. Youngsters say so often, "There's no use in going to Mother or Father, for what they advise never works out." We had better be slow about *telling* them what to do. *Listen*, offer suggestions, help them think their problem through for themselves; but don't flatly tell them unless there is an emergency and you have to. If you work things out with them in this way they will come back again to talk things over.

## They Grow Socially

My small son said to me one afternoon, "I want a child to play with, you don't know what I want to play." I was seated on the ground by him, and as far as I could get physically I was on his level; but I really didn't know what he wanted to play and couldn't enter fully into his thinking. I was too much older. All the way through life there is this longing for the kind of friend who knows what we want to play, who can think and work, and laugh and cry on our plane. This urge to find a congenial spirit is almost overwhelming in the teen-ager. He wants a chum, a best friend, someone with whom he can share his new ideas, feelings, and experiences; someone in whom he can confide these strange new hopes and fears, who will confirm his judgments about life and people, who will give affection for affection, who will appreciate him and make him feel secure, approved. Their conversation seems to us to be about such trivial things—the last basketball game, the current movie, a joke just heard over the radio, the new boy or girl in school, the unfair teacher, and so it goes. Daughter talks endlessly over the phone while we wonder about the long distance call trying to get through to us. One moment she is completely serious, the next all giggles. What can be important enough to talk about so long? Will she never stop? It is the very breath of life to her. She has some new idea which calls for more talk. Be patient, your call can't mean as much as this!

These youngsters normally choose their friends from those on the same socio-economic level. Where they live, the clothes they wear, the things they have, their ability, their common interests—football, dramatics, dancing—these are the conditioning factors. Your daughter who has grown all these years in your home ought to be able to choose her friends wisely. If you are in doubt about her close friends, to make fun of them, to criticize, will hurt her deeply and may only stir her to defend them, increase her loyalty. Invite them in, so she may see them in her home setting. If they are not the right kind, that may be enough.

A sudden, intensive devotion to an older woman, or a friend the same age, a "crush," is rather common with girls. The teacher may embody an ideal which she has been gradually creating, she may not find mother or father responsive to her affection, she hasn't been attractive to boys, she doesn't make friends easily, so she gives herself to her teacher, or to another girl. This may narrow her opportunities for fellowship, may result in severe hurt, if her beloved growing weary of her attentions drops her; so crushes aren't to be encouraged. Yet unless they are very absorbing, they shouldn't cause much worry if she has other interests. It is another stage in her life to be outgrown.

Not only does the boy and girl in this period find a friend, but they become part of a *group*. Boys and girls may be separate, as in Boy and Girl Scouts, or fraternities and sororities in high school or college, or they may be together in informal or organized social groups.

The crowd with which they run will have probably six or a

dozen boys and girls living within a few blocks of each other, attending the same school, with the same socio-economic background. They may move from house to house, on the porch in the summer, inside in the winter, watching television, listening to the radio or records, dancing, talking, raiding the refrigerator, wandering to the drugstore. It doesn't seem very exciting or educational to us but it means everything to them. It is their world in which they are at home, where they can talk as they please, express their doubts and uncertainties without fear of being misunderstood, and get off their chest their gripes about teachers and parents, sure that sympathetic ears will listen, for all are going through the same experiences, often unhappy, in the world controlled by adults.

In a sense the crowd is their defense against this world of older people in which they have to live much of the time, and in which they are not altogether at home. With each other they are relaxed, secure, approved. Some of them now get their feeling of security from the peer group rather than from their homes. It gives them a grand sense of "belonging."

From the give-and-take of their free fellowship in their crowd they learn to get along with people, the kind of conduct that is approved and disapproved. Rough edges are rounded off, social skills are acquired, self-understanding is gained, for a group may force one of its number to "get wise" to himself. They are preparing themselves for the adult world into which another step or two will bring them. The pity of it is that a select group may become snobbish, and those who are left out may feel lonely, inferior, resentful. Not a few are in no crowd. Only the heart of one left out can know its own bitterness.

The group pattern is almost compulsive in its power over clothes, speech, amusements, and some types of conduct. One must be like the group to be popular, to have status. A girl will say and almost mean it, "I'd rather die than be out of style." Style for her is what is the vogue in her group at that moment. A fad starts and, as someone said, spreads through the group as rapidly as water from an overturned tumbler races across the table. If it is pedal pushers, blue jeans, or Bermuda shorts, she wears them though they may be uncomfortable and add nothing to the looks of her type of figure. Mother may not like them, father may be vocal in his disapproval, small brother may tease, but "everybody's wearing them," so she must conform. Ridicule from her group, she just can't take.

As parents we should try to know something about the crowd, their names, where they live, who their parents are, their general outlook on life. We must open our homes to our children's friends. Some time ago I was in a home of wealth which had been built with the children in mind. On the top floor there was a gymnasium with a basketball court—not full-size. In the basement, a swimming pool that could be heated in winter, a bowling alley, and a pool table. In the yard was a cement tennis court with the edges turned up so that it could be flooded in the winter for a skating rink. That home was the hangout of the crowd. More recently I visited a family whose house cost hardly a tenth as much, yet there was a rumpus room in a semi-basement. It had a coke-bar, a pingpong table, a television set, and comfortable chairs. Father and mother always knew where their two girls were.

A room of that kind may be beyond our means; but we probably have a radio, a record player, perhaps a television set, a room that will do if it is rearranged a bit and the family withdraws almost immediately. We can furnish cookies, and cokes or ginger ale. Don't let us fool ourselves into believing that they like us better if we learn their slang—this is their world, not ours. Fortunately, if we try to, it changes so often we have to give up. "Ephemeral slang, born yesterday, dead tomorrow, but so alive today," cannot be mastered by an adult. They may like to meet us as they come in and go away, but unless we are needed for a season to play the piano or help them sing, they are happier if left to themselves. Though some of them may run in to see us now and then if we have a friendly heart, we are simply not of their generation no matter how we dress, or try to talk their lingo.

If the influence of this particular group isn't good, it may be we can find another for our youngsters. Just to pull them out of their crowd and leave them stranded, alone, may do them more harm than the influence of their group, unless it is almost wholly bad. If they have been happy in their home, if love has dwelt there and the Lord Christ has been its true center, then the home can hold against the group in the things that matter most. Real growth may come through their experience with others as values are sifted out, ideals seen more clearly. Strength may be born out of the conflict with the group.

The Church may have a chance with boys and girls of this age if it can provide an attractive place for them to hang out, interesting things for them to do, and above all vital young leaders. Havighurst and Taba found that while sixteen-year-olds may create an imaginary, composite ideal from reading and contact with people, as "the person I would like to be like," many of them choose "an attractive, visible adult" who is in the twenties.[5]

We used to think that altruism, an unselfish attitude toward life, was as certainly a part of an adolescent's life as down on his upper lip; both being a part of the pattern of life given him by his inheritance. Now we know that it is largely learned from the kind of home in which he matures, and the kind of group with which he associates. We need the church groups, sane, full of fun, giving time to study and service under stimulating leadership, to offset the selfishness and cruelty that the wrong kind of group or crowd creates, and fosters.

## They Should Have a Real Measure of Freedom

Our students have put questionnaires asking, "Whom do you want to be like?" into the hands of hundreds of boys and girls of different ages. Many adolescents reply, "I want to be like myself!" The teen-ager feels a new sense of selfhood, and has a strong desire for independence. One boy, not among those we questioned, said that as he was walking past a store he caught a glimpse of himself in its big window and there swept through him the overwhelming sense that "I am I." Hamlin Garland tells us that one day he said to his father, "Father, I want a hat." His father reminded him that he had a cap which was sufficient. Then, something happened inside of the lad, for he drew himself up and declared in a tone that was so different it scared him, "Father, I am going to have a hat." The wise father, seeing that he was dealing with a new boy, answered readily, "All right, my son, if that's the way you feel about it, you shall have a hat."[6] It may not happen so suddenly as that, but during this period there may come a declaration of independence, if not defiance. It isn't surprising; for he is big and strong with a new sense of power pulsing through him, he can think and knows that some wisdom is his. He has been accepted on an equal basis by a friend, and has the support of his group. Quite naturally he wants to be listened to and respected by his parents. It is well that this is so, for one of the necessities of growing up is "emancipation from the home." Many are the books and articles written about "apron strings," which advise that they must be gradually untied by mother and father. If we are not wise enough to do this our boys and girls may become passive marionettes, moving only at our directions; or in rebellion may break the cords, throw off all parental restraint, and go their own way. In either case both we and they are hurt.

We would not have them dependent, timid souls, who can't mix easily with their fellows in the neighborhood or at school, who can't stand on their own feet as they grow older, who when the going gets tough in business or marriage must run home to Mother. They can never be happy, and we shall know only disappointment as they fail to realize the high hopes we have had for them. As we begin to be aware of their new powers we may become a little frightened and pull back on the reins; but to hold them so tight that they feel that the only way they can have any freedom is to jerk them out of our hands and run off, may mean disaster to them and heartache to us.

We are in difficulty. We love our children, we are concerned about what is best for them, we know that we should relax our hold. Yet we have put so much of our very lives into them, we enjoy them so greatly, that we are jealous of the outside world that would take them from us and leave us somewhat empty-handed with our work largely gone—and empty-hearted, for each child has his particular place which nothing else can fill. So in shortsightedness and selfishness we draw the strings tighter, and try to make our youngsters' bondage more attractive.

In our better moments we want them to choose their own clothes, their friends, their ways of having a good time; we know that they grow through deciding things for themselves, that they have to make mistakes to learn. But they seem so young, so immature, they were so innocent yesterday, there is so much evil in the world. So many horrible things happen to young people today. That story on the front page of the morning paper about a hot-rod car skidding into a tree on a curve, and killing a seventeen-year-old boy and the sixteen-year-old girl who was with him, sent cold shivers down our spines. We don't want our children to be hurt, to get in the wrong crowd. Believing with Paul that "bad company ruins good morals,"[7] we yearn to protect them. Our fears defeat our good judgment and we hold them close.

The last book we read may have advised a gradual loosening of the reins in harmony with the growth of their ability to manage themselves. Our timing must be just right. If we lag behind their capacity to take over their own lives we hurt them. If we run ahead of their ability to assume responsibility and give them too much freedom too early, they are in difficulty. We know this is sound advice, but why wasn't the writer more specific, why didn't he tell us just what to do and when? Even as we utter this mental protest we know that no outsider could give us such definite guidance. We realize that this problem can be solved only by our own "blood, sweat, and tears." The will to do is half the battle!

## They Should Have Understanding Parents

The development of a helpful relationship with our sons and daughters depends so much on our *attitude*. Tommy says, "Half our problems in the home would be solved if we just knew Daddy would be reasonable." Out of his life with his group, the games he has played, has come a sense of fairness which he feels is violated if his father condemns, or issues commands without giving a moment's consideration to his viewpoint.

We must discover and talk over with them the "sticking points," without raising our voices, or losing our tempers, as graciously and fairly as we discuss moot questions with our own friends. This takes *time*. A common complaint is that Mother or Daddy "never seems to have the time to sit down and talk to me." It takes more than time. They expect us to be intelligent. It would be wise for us to try to think through the disagreements that have been found most common between parents and children, so that when we face them they will not take us by surprise and arouse our emotions to such an extent that we cannot look at them objectively. A good many studies made from the standpoint of both parents and teen-agers warn us to expect certain problems which occur rather frequently. Here are only a few of them: "going out on school nights, the time you get home at night, grades at school, using the family car, choosing friends, spending money, jobs at home."

It is difficult for us to be reasonable, as our children would judge it, about these and other matters. We are much older than they are—in the forties or even older, when they are in their teens. They are so vital, so active, and we are beginning to slow down. We simply cannot believe that we ever had that much energy, did so many different things in a day. Our memories of that period are blurred. One mother who had kept a very detailed diary of her adolescent years read it when her daughter reached that period. This made for a much happier relationship as she found to her astonishment that she had the same driving energy which, exhibited now in her daughter, had created tension between them. What a difference it might make if we had old diaries to consult!

Could it be that a part of our trouble in dealing reasonably with our youngsters grows out of jealousy? Mother whose beauty has faded a bit, and whose body has rounded out a little too much, may look with envy at her slim, lovely daughter. Father may not be wholly happy when he can't cover the court with the speed of yesterday and his vigorous son takes his measure in tennis.

Then, too, our culture has changed; life has speeded up in the twenty to forty years which separate us from our children. They consider us stupid, old-fashioned, woefully behind the times; we regard them as over-modern, reckless, foolish. It irritates rather than helps for us to say, "We didn't *have* that when we were your age." Of course we didn't; "that" may not have been in existence then, and if it was available our parents didn't have the money that we have. "We didn't *do* that when we were sixteen!" Maybe not, for the community frowned upon it then and our parents had an authority that isn't ours. They are thinking of what *their* group has and does *now*. If we are wise we shall find out, for it is only then that we can have a meeting of minds. Some things seemed so wrong yesterday, today this judgment may be questioned. Take dancing, for example. For more than thirty years in classes studying youth at Union Seminary and the General Assembly's Training School, I have asked more than a thousand students whether or not they had danced—little, or much, or not at all; and what was the effect—harmful, mixed, neutral, or helpful. Years ago very few had danced at all and they were not sure the experience was helpful. In the last few years the great majority of these young men and women, the leaders-to-be in our Church, reported that they had danced, and with rare exceptions said the experience had been helpful. Several who had not danced wrote of the way in which not being allowed to dance had made it difficult for them to associate normally with the other sex, and had given them a feeling of being left out of the crowd. Even now they felt inhibited in a group, and had a lingering sense of inferiority.

How well I remembered, as I read their papers, how forlorn I was as a little boy when my whole crowd went to dancing school on Thursday afternoons and I was left alone with nothing to do, and how out-of-place and embarrassed I was as I grew older when I didn't know how to dance and didn't dance, when for most of my crowd at college and during my vacations at a summer resort dancing was a major pastime. I had never heard of an "inferiority complex," but I had one. To this day I am not always comfortable in a mixed group. I don't see how I could have gotten along except for the support given me in my home, and the ability to hold my own in several sports with anyone in my group. Yesterday we thought only of the possible moral harm in dancing, and not of what might happen deep in the personality of boys and girls for whom dancing was prohibited.

I am not advising dancing as the best form of recreation. I am quite aware of its dangers for I have talked them out with my own children and other young people. I realize also how it limits conversation, and keeps people from having to do any creative thinking about their amusements. Without using one's mind at all the rug can be rolled back and the record player turned on. But certainly we can't say that one of the distinctive marks of a young Christian should be that he does not dance. Too long we have majored in negatives. It is often easier for a young person to defend himself against what we have thought of as moral harm, than against emotional crippling. Doesn't an experience that prevents his full and happy development through association with friends have in it something of moral wrong? Our Lord laid stress on the positive and came "that they might have life, and that they might have it more abundantly."[8]

Probably as parents we should rethink our values. Some of us are severely conditioned by the homes in which we grew up, and reached conclusions from our group experience without having really thought them through. To say, "Mother knows best," when we won't, or can't, give any valid reasons for our position may only result in our youngsters discounting our ability or our honesty, and doing with a bad conscience what we have forbidden. Sometimes they have to raise an issue to make sure that they are not wholly bound to us. It may be smoking, or outlandish clothes, or a freakish hair-do. Regardless of how sharply our ideas may differ, we must maintain a happy and an understanding relationship with them.

We can't control them any longer by force; tears only embarrass them, and make them wonder about *our* maturity; we wouldn't stoop to threats, they are useless anyway. We must convince them that we respect them as persons, and will be reasonable as we talk over their problems with them. The only way they can be safe in a world like this, and of help to others, will be for them to give their full, joyous loyalty to ideals in which we have helped them believe.

Much is being written these days about the family council —a meeting of its members at a set time for the discussion of anything that might be of interest, with complete freedom granted to the youngest to voice what is on his mind. Sometimes it is planned for and minutes are kept. But whether or not there is a formal gathering of the clan, the spirit of the home should be such that at any time permissive group discussion could be a part of its fellowship, and all could feel free to go to father or mother with a joy to share, or a matter in which help is needed. It is in such homes that we find boys and girls who say from happy hearts, "My parents are understanding," "My parents treat me as their equal in all family discussions and problems," "My opinion concerning matters of interest, family or otherwise, is frequently requested."⁹

While we may be having our difficulties now, and at times be almost in despair, if ours is a democratic Christian home we can look forward to the day, not so far off, when we shall have a mature, happy relationship with these fine grown men and women who such a short while ago as youngsters in our homes tested our patience to the limit. They are appreciative now as they could never have been before of the sacrifices we made for them, the sleepless nights and anxious days, the self-denials that sent them to camp, and put money in the bank for their college education. They are struggling to raise their own family, a new understanding has come out of experience, and spontaneous letters are written expressing gratitude for all that we had and did together, and wonder that there was ever money enough for shoes and food! This will be our rich reward. We can live by hope!

## They Should Have a Chance for Fellowship with the Other Sex

The crowd means so much to a young person, because he finds in it members of the other sex. The strong sense of independence felt in this period is in part due to the fact that the boy through his association with girls has a new sense of being a man; and the girl realizes as she has not done before that she is a woman. This growing interest in the opposite sex is another stage through which our youngsters pass on their way to that mature relationship which will be a mark of their adult life.

Small boys and girls play together without much sense of sex differences; but in later childhood they pull apart and girls run with girls, and boys give their loyalty to their chums, or to the gang.

A few more years, and boys and girls begin to feel almost a compulsive interest in each other. In the nineteen-thirties a girl fourteen answered our question, "Are you going with boys?" with the words, "Not yet!" A fifteen-year-old girl said, "Just beginning," and a sixteen-year-older, "Every chance I get." Their attitudes were rather typical of the girls of those years. In the nineteen-fifties they may start going with boys earlier. Life has speeded up since the War, and some parents are hurrying their youngsters along. Others caught in the fast-moving current can do little about it. Is this wise? For a girl to have a formal dress and orchids at thirteen or fourteen, and to experience most of the thrills of a full social life that would normally come later, may mean that as she grows older life goes flat, and nothing will serve as a fillip except a cup that brings bitterness as it is drained.

This interest in the other sex quickens in girls a year or two earlier than it does in boys, and among girls and boys there is a wide variation in the time it begins and in its intensity. There are boys who are absorbed in sports or in making a boat or a model airplane, and there are girls who find their life in music, or art, or the world of literature; who like to write and can.

The turning of a girl toward a boy, or a boy toward a girl, springs out of their very natures. When God created both man and woman, this desire and need were born in them. It brought the family into being, it ensures the perpetuation of the race. We must encourage and guide it.

Two Purdue University professors by means of the Purdue

Opinion Panel questioned 2500 high school youths about dating. They were asked from a list of twenty-three items considered objectionable on a date to decide, first, which items were more characteristic of each sex, and, second, which items they felt to be personal problems to themselves. The item, "Is shy, self-conscious, or ill-at-ease," was first on the list as each sex judged the other, and as both boys and girls thought of their own problems in dating.[10]

As they first reach out for each other the strangeness of the feeling, at times its violence, may make them self-conscious, awkward, even afraid. A boy may not know what to say, or what to do, or where to take a girl on their first date. If he has no "line," and she can find nothing to say, their suffering may be excruciating. To sit or walk in silence is terrible. It is not quite so bad if one is driving. He can give his attention to the road and the wheel. She can watch the changing scenery. A failure at the very beginning may send the girl home in tears, and make the boy hesitate about trying again. The hurt of an initial bungling may go deep, and be lasting.

As I recall, it was Josiah Royce who said, "One cannot do expertly what one has not done before." Boy and girl behavior has to be learned like any other skill. What a blessing if life in the home has prepared them for this vital new experience. An understanding older brother or sister can give them pointers. They have already been along the way. Parents may have smoothed the path by freeing them to talk from their childhood days, by opening the home to their friends through the years, and by making it a place now where the crowd delights to come. A mother suddenly alerted to the need of her daughter can't do for her in a day what she should have been doing for a decade or more.

An only child, or a child in a home where interests are not

shared, where nobody talks, into which no visitors ever come, may find happy association with the other sex exceedingly difficult.

Someone must help them. A group in the church, a young couple who can bring this boy and girl together in their home, may be their salvation. This urge is God-implanted; if it is blocked, life knows one of its greatest frustrations. There are leaders of youth who feel strongly that lack of an opportunity for dating, or unhappy experiences on dates, may result in personality defects; whereas joyous association with the other sex may help correct maladjustments which have developed in earlier years.

Going with a crowd, double and triple dating, may be of the greatest value to the shy, inexperienced boy and girl. It makes them feel more at ease in each other's presence, helps them overcome awkwardness, teaches them how to behave as they watch those more skilled. It may prevent a boy's relationship with a girl from becoming too absorbing on a physical level. Heavy petting is less likely to occur if two or three couples are together at a bowling alley, skating rink, or football game, than if two are alone in a car, or in someone's living room.

Sometimes we make it harder for a son or a daughter by teasing, laughing about "puppy love." It all seems so funny. Some remembered incident in our own experience now strikes us as ridiculous. We have forgotten the agony that we felt at the time. It is so serious for them. Billy may say, "There isn't another girl like Mary in the world, so beautiful, so smart, so talented. This is for always." He means it. He is in love with her. He is also in love with love.

Next month it may be Susie about whom he raves. Six months later it is Patty who is the perfect girl for him, and she may be. For by running with the crowd and seeing many girls, by going steady, falling, oh, so desperately in love with one and then another, he is learning to understand better himself and his own needs, to find what it is in a girl that he really likes, and what in her draws out the best in him. So little by little he prepares himself to discover in Patty the girl to whom he can give himself permanently, with whom he wants to live forever.

Suppose he has had no such opportunity through the middle teens, no chance to meet and know rather well a number of girls. How vulnerable he will be to the charms of the first attractive girl who comes along! He knows no other by whom he can measure her. He has no way of judging whether or not his love will hold should he meet later another interesting member of the other sex who has predatory propensities.

Could our teasing be caused by *jealousy*, a hidden desire to make him unhappy because he has hurt us by seeming forgetfulness in his exclusive interest in someone else? Are we critical of each girl he chooses, hoping that he will find none of them attractive enough to lure him away from us? Such selfish love, if successful in keeping him from finding a girl with whom he can be happy and establish a home of his own, will probably result in a life of misery for him, and for us, and in the end he turns on us in hate for the wrong we have done him.

Perhaps *fear* makes us try to keep our youngsters from going with the other sex. Yet we should be unhappy if our boys and girls are not popular. With one part of us we want them to have dates; with another we are concerned about what might happen when they are together. So many lurid stories are written about parked cars, roadhouses, petting and necking and promiscuous relations. We have heard enough about Dr. Kinsey and his findings to make us afraid.

## They Should Have Sex Education

It is when we get to this place in our thinking that we realize that our boys and girls must be given an understanding of the meaning of sex in their lives. They are very conscious of the physical changes they are experiencing, of the primary and secondary sex characteristics which are so evident, and of the accompanying emotions which are so upsetting.

In *Profile of Youth*, a survey of teen-agers conducted by members of the *Ladies Home Journal* staff, it is stated that the question, "What, according to high school students, is the most important personal problem facing them today?" was answered, "What should we do about sex?"*

To answer that question they need *knowledge*, so wisely and cleanly and adequately given as to prevent, remove, or allay fear and shame and curiosity. It is hard to believe that in these sophisticated days, past the middle of the twentieth century, some girls are left in such ignorance that they are frightened by the onset of menstruation, and boys by nocturnal emissions. Yet it is so. Boys are often terrified by the thought that masturbation, which is such a common practice, usually short-lived, will result in blocked physical development, or in insanity.

Girls, especially, are left to approach this period believing that sex is bad in itself, with the result that they are possessed by feelings of shame and guilt, simply because the desire is experienced. This may make them unhappy now, and may result in serious difficulty when they are married. Curiosity is strong in the pubescent years—interest in anything unknown and new. Add to this the dynamic of sex, and their de-

---

* From *Profile of Youth*, edited by Maureen Daly, copyright, 1949, 1950, 1951, by Curtis Publishing Company. Published by J. B. Lippincott Company.

sire for knowledge in this realm becomes acute. Curiosity thwarted is curiosity whetted; so if we do not give them facts in a wholesome way, they may seek answers to their questions from poisonous sources.

We should enable them to know that this urge is a *natural* part of life at this period, as natural as the desire for food and drink, and as natural for the girl as for the boy.

We would have them understand that it is a *strong* urge, more pervasive in the girl, involving her whole body, and more localized in the boy; that it is more easily and quickly excited in the boy, especially by physical contact; and that when it is aroused it may become overwhelming. It is stronger in some persons than in others, and in the same person more uncontrollable at certain times than at others. For both boy and girl to know this may help them to be on their guard against going, in their physical intimacies, beyond the point of no return.

We should see that they realize that this is a *holy* urge. They must understand that it isn't merely a physical desire, but that it is a part of, and involves, the whole personality. When the "Maker of heaven and earth" formed both man and woman for each other He took them into partnership with Himself for the perpetuation of the race, for the creation of other persons—body, mind, and spirit. It is a glorious and awesome ability with which He endowed us. It is a responsibility to be undertaken only by two people who, with an understanding of its meaning, give themselves in love to each other in a fellowship more intimate and complete than any other they can know.

The late William Temple, Archbishop of Canterbury, who, according to Sir Winston Churchill, was one of the four or five ablest men in the British Empire, and who was revered by those who knew him best for his "sheer goodness," made a notable contribution to our thinking on this subject. Dr. Iremonger, in his biography of Bishop Temple, states that in an address made in July, 1943, he lifted the whole matter to the height from which he surveyed every department of human life and where two thoughts were dominant—the sacredness of personality and the fact of God. After speaking of the respect due from all men for another's personality, the Bishop went on to say, "It is just the same with sex relationships. To use that function of our nature as an opportunity of passing amusement always involves treating another person as a plaything or a toy. That is destructive of the freedom we are fighting to maintain, for the heart of that freedom is the dignity of personality. But here, even more than in the other case, the religious background makes all the difference in the world. There is nothing nasty about sex as God has made it; there is no reason why it should not be spoken of in a natural and matter-of-fact way; but it must be treated with respect and even with reverence, because it is the means by which men and women are enabled to act on behalf of God in the creation of His children, which is why parents are said to procreate. The reason for not joking about sex is exactly the same as for not joking about the Holy Communion. It is not that the subject is nasty, but that it is sacred, and to joke about it is profanity. Moreover it is the point at which the spiritual and the physical come into closest interplay, and this no doubt is why moralists normally take it as the example of the moral struggle. Sexual sin is not the only sort of sin nor the worst kind of sin; the supreme sin and the fountainhead of all the others is pride, not lust. But if we let this function be used for our pleasure and amusement we are spoiling one of the most splendid things in the world."[11]

*Knowledge is not enough.* Bishop Temple makes it plain that we must go beyond any statement of the facts about sex. The most convincing expression of this truth I have seen is in a little book, *Christianity and Sex,* by Dr. Richard C. Cabot, who as professor in the Harvard Medical School, and as chief of the medical staff of Massachusetts General Hospital, can speak with authority. Let me quote at length again.

"I have been dealing for forty years with medical students; as a teacher and practitioner of medicine I have had to do with some thousands of them, and have been pretty intimate with a good many hundreds. Medical students, by reason of their studies, have to know the facts of anatomy, physiology, and disease on which many of the teachings of what is called sex hygiene appear to depend. These students know such facts better than I could present them to anyone concerned merely for morality; but I have never found that their knowledge of these facts made them any more chaste than other people, or any less so—rather it left them just about the average of men. Now, if the full knowledge of facts could hold people straight and make them behave themselves, medical students ought to be an ideal body of men. But they are not. Next to medical students, nurses, I suppose, know more of these facts than any other group, yet I have never found that nurses as a body behave any better than the average of the groups from which they were drawn. If a knowledge of facts could make people behave themselves, medical people generally would certainly be the leaders of the world in this matter; but they are not. We have, therefore, a sufficient answer to any who believe that knowledge of facts and the resulting fear of consequences, dread of disease and shame, are powerful motives for good behavior in this field." [12]

*Ideals* must be built into our boys and girls—ideals not only about sex, but about life as a whole, which are determined, as Dr. Temple holds, by their conception of God and persons. If they are children of God they cannot deal with others, who are His children too, as if they were only bodies. They cannot use them in utter selfishness for a momentary satisfaction on a physical level. They are of infinite value as through God's grace they are immortal spirits, and must be respected as such.

If we could help our boys and girls to see the sacredness of personality because of its relationship to God, it would be difficult for them to engage in the kind of prolonged petting which majors in bodily intimacies and measures a date by the physical thrills experienced.

It is our responsibility too, as has been indicated already, to give them as full and happy a life as possible. Friends, interesting activities, a home in which people are respected and in which they are loved and find joy, will help them solve their sex problems. Sometimes boys and girls major in the physical because they haven't much else to do, have few interests. Some, because they are insecure, unhappy at home, find satisfaction in this kind of indulgence. Possibly the roots of their trouble are not sexual, but go deep into their failure to make any real adjustment to life. They do not understand what they are for, and have no enticing goals before them. They can't get along with people, and each day brings them new frustrations and anxieties. Sex is their way of escape, or a means of feeling important through their mastery of someone else.

It might seem from what has been said that sex education should begin when these new urges appear. It starts really with the attitude we have developed toward sex before the child is born. If for us sex is natural and holy, we shall not be afraid when that exploratory hand touches his genitals as innocently as any other part of his body, and cry, "You are a bad boy to do that, stop it!" Our words may not say that, but the atmosphere we create does, and we start him on the way to thinking that sex is something to be ashamed of or to fear.

If we are adjusted ourselves we shall answer his first questions unemotionally and factually. They may begin as early as two. Most children start asking them around four or five, when they question us about so many other things. Sex education in the sense of imparting knowledge begins when the first intelligent question is asked. It usually doesn't demand more than a simple answer. If we could just get a child's viewpoint, and not impose our adult thinking upon his limited needs and so pace the information we give at the rate of his interest! "Mummie, where did I come from?" "Here it is," we say, and try to think of an elaborate answer, when a simple, truthful statement, "You grew inside Mother's body," may satisfy him for some time, and be all that he is prepared to take in. If our own attitude in meeting his early questions is natural, unmarked by any reaction which would indicate that his question was indelicate or out of place; if we do not blush, are not solemn, then he will come to us again as his mind develops and he wants to know more. So little by little the story of how he was conceived and born is before him. Better still, our wholesome attitude toward sex becomes his.

Two distinguished psychiatrists associated with Temple University Medical School assure us that when sex questions are dealt with early and frankly by his parents, "it denotes to the child an acceptance of himself, an acceptance of his body and of the impulses of his body."[13] As a result he can accept his body and its impulses without shame or fear. The problem of sex education, like so many others, should be largely solved before adolescence.

If we do not give them early the knowlege they need, they

will get ideas of some sort, often in garbled or hurtful form. It is not a question of the right kind of education, or no education; but of the right kind or the wrong kind. If we do not educate them, their companions will. If we wait until later they have no protection against misinformation and wrong attitudes, and it is harder for us and for them to begin to think together about this subject. When they are aware of the new emotions they are experiencing, it may be quite embarrassing for both of us.

But whether we try to instruct them early or wait until later, this is the parents' duty—fathers' as truly as mothers'! The head of the department of biology at the University of Richmond lectures to the freshman class each year on sex. He asked one class, "Whom would you rather have had give you the information I have given you?" One student answered, "Of all the men I know, I would rather have had my father do it." The great majority of the students agreed with him.

High school students feel, according to a *Profile of Youth*, that "help must come chiefly from home." "They need," so the authors say, "the freedom to talk with someone, preferably someone at home."* That freedom is determined by the kind of relationship parents maintain with their children. As girls are closer to their mothers than boys are to their fathers, they are more apt to discuss intimate matters with their mothers than boys are with their fathers. Whether or not we give our children sex instruction, we are giving them, whether we wish to or not, whether we know it or not, sex attitudes.

## They Should Have Privacy

They need privacy in this period. Their yearning for it is part of their new sense of independence, their desire to break

---

* Maureen Daly, *op. cit.*

the apron strings. We have to restrain our curiosity about their comings and goings. "Where were you this afternoon? What did you do? Whom were you with?" have fallen so naturally from our lips for so long that it is hard to remember that asked now such questions may be regarded almost as impertinence. If we do not press them, our youngsters may be happy to confide in us when they are in the right mood. Young people complain that parents are inquisitive about their phone calls, even open their letters, or if they dare not go that far, recognize the handwriting and count them!

We have been told that one should not have a child unless he can give him a room of his own. That would certainly limit the number of children in some families! But a *teen-ager,* if possible, should have his own room. A girl wants a place where she can put her corsage ribbons, pennants, ticket stubs, pictures of movie stars, and a thousand things that have no value to anyone else. She wants a sanctuary where she can be alone, to dream her dreams about dates with her new hero, it may be to cry over disappointments, to write in her diary the secrets she cannot share with her best friend. To have to room with a younger sister who teases and is inquisitive is torment.

A boy likes to be by himself too, to have his own room where he can think the long, long thoughts of youth, work on some hobby—stamps, radio, chemistry, records. He wants a haven to which he can bring his friends, and where they can laugh and talk hours on end without being disturbed.

## They Should Be Trusted

Just as trust is basic in the relation of husband and wife, so it is between parents and children. "My parents are always suspicious of everything I do," laments a teen-ager. "I'm getting to the place that I'm not caring much any more if they keep doubting me."[14] How different is the feeling of a boy who writes, "My parents take my word as something of value. If Mother or Father asks me something regarding my activities, my answer is accepted without any hesitation."[15] How much better, even, if they trust him to do the right thing, to live up to the standard set by life in the home, without continually exhorting him, or questioning him about his conduct! Such trust brings to the fore the best in him, and makes him, regardless of group pressure, purpose to deserve his parents' confidence.

Years ago I heard a man, president of a college, distinguished for his character and his rich service to Church and State, tell of an experience he had with his father the day before he left for college. His father invited him to take a walk with him. "Well," he thought, "Dad will now lecture me on the temptations I shall face at college, drinking and gambling and sex. He will talk to me about studying hard, living up to the opportunities for self-improvement and being helpful. He will urge me to be honest and faithful to every duty." He rather dreaded the experience. But to his surprise the walk was a pleasant one. His father chatted interestingly about his own college days. There were stories about hazing and athletics and fraternities; helpful hints about how to get along with upper classmen. The boy was thrown wholly off his guard. As they turned and started home his father put his hand on the lad's shoulder. "Here it comes," he thought, and began to build his defenses. But his father was a wise man. Looking him straight in the eye, his father said, "Son, I just want you to know that whatever happens your mother and I trust you." That was all. It was enough! That boy determined then and there, with steel wrought into his will, that no matter what the cost he would never violate such trust. He never did!

# 6

## Love Interacts

*I*N the last century John Bright, one of England's most eminent statesmen, stated, "The nation rests on the cottage." Early in this century Sir Edward Lyttleton, headmaster of the famous Eton School, wrote a book on the home, which he called *The Cornerstone of Education*. More recently Dr. Nels Ferré said, "Win the family for Christian living and the world is won."[1] Today, a thousand voices are raised to tell us that the family is the primary social unit, upon which depend for their life the State, and the school, and the Church. Mr. Edgar Hoover, head of the FBI, makes the sweeping statement, "The home is the citadel of American life. If the home is lost, all is lost."

The importance of the home for the school, the nation, and the Church can readily be seen. It is evident that the home has life almost exclusively within its borders during the early years, which are so meaningful that Horace Bushnell expressed his "solemn conviction" that the first three years of a child's life are more important, as a general fact, in their bearing upon education and character, than all the years of discipline that may come thereafter.[2] Of course, that was nearly a hundred years ago, but the observation is as up-to-date as if you had heard it over the radio only a few minutes ago. Some years ago Dr. Frank Richardson, in his *Parenthood and the Newer Psychology*, claimed that the emotional difficulties which involve so many of us in later life have their roots in our experiences in these early years, and that the main character trends which make us what we are now were largely fixed before we were six years old.[3] A host of more recent writers agree with him.

It is inevitable that these years should have so meaningful a place in life, for they are the foundational years. They stand at the beginning of life. Quite naturally Dr. Arnold Gesell, formerly head of the Child Development Clinic at Yale University, says they have "The autocracy of priority, they come first." All life is built upon them. What you put into them you put into all the subsequent years.

It is, however, more serious than that. For what you put into these first years will condition and color everything that comes into life thereafter. We are so created that we can learn only on the basis of our previous knowledge and experience. In 1924, while in Korea lecturing on religious education, I was told by a missionary that a little Korean boy, when he encountered for the first time a man on a bicycle, rushed home and cried out, "Mother, I just saw a man riding down the street on a great big pair of spectacles." Spectacles are a common sight in that country, for the older men wear them with pride. The boy was only interpreting the new, as he had to do, in the light of the familiar.

What holds for the realm of general knowledge is true, also, for religion. Kate Douglas Wiggin, one of the really great kindergartners of yesterday, makes this plain in the story of a little crippled boy named Patsy. His teacher tried to give him a sense of security, and courage for life, by revealing to him that God was his Father. When she had finished what she thought was a clear and moving presentation of the heart and mind of God, the boy exclaimed, "If God's like earthly fathers, I don't want any of Him. Mine kicked me down three flights of stairs, and I've never been well since." Any attempt to teach a boy truth, whether it be secular or religious, must rest on, and be colored by, what has become his in the early years in the home.

Furthermore, there are certain so-called laws or principles of social psychology which make it clear that life in the family *during these early years, and later,* will influence us profoundly.

## I. The Principle of Suggestion

There is a tendency in us to accept uncritically and make a part of our thinking what we hear other people say. The effectiveness of suggestion is dependent on a number of factors. It is determined by the *amount, character, and organization of our knowledge* in a particular field. If our facts are few, and our experience is meager, and we have built what we know into no clear pattern, then our minds are wide open to anything another may say. If a man were to talk to me about banking or merchandising, I should be ready to accept whatever he might advise. But if our conversation turns to education, a field in which I have been teaching for thirty years, I not only have a considerable amount of knowledge but I have built it into a framework against which I can quickly check his ideas, and I shall be inclined to do just that.

The power of suggestion is conditioned to some extent by the *prestige* of the one speaking. There is what we call acquired prestige, which belongs to a man by virture of his position; and personal prestige, which he has as a result of his own attractiveness. The reason the speeches of Churchill during the War were so tremendous in their effect was in part his prestige. He had acquired prestige—he was the real head of the British Commonwealth of Nations. He had personal prestige—he was compelling as a man in his courage and dynamic qualities, and in his ability to put together the simple words of our mother tongue in such a way that they marched before us like an army with banners.

Suggestion is more effective when it is *indirect*. When we feel that another is deliberately trying to bring us to his way of thinking, we are apt to resist, to build up our defenses against him. Our ego is involved and we begin to argue on the other side. Something within will not let us surrender. Even if he seems to defeat us in reasoning, we will not yield. But a chance remark of his slips under our guard—we really haven't put it up—and enters our minds with persuasive power. In an address on "The Imponderables of Medicine," before the Richmond Academy of Medicine, the late Dr. John Finney of Baltimore, one of America's most distinguished surgeons— a brigadier general in the First World War, and a man of great personal magnetism—told a story which illustrates the effectiveness of indirect suggestion. A colleague sent him a patient who, he felt, needed a slight operation. Dr. Finney confirmed the diagnosis. But when he told the man what was before him, he said at once, "Doctor, you can't operate on me, for if you do I am going to die." His fear was so extreme that Dr. Finney phoned his fellow physician, and only after lengthy consultation did they decide to perform the operation. Meanwhile he tried to convince his patient that there was no danger. He told him that his physical condition was all that could be asked, that the operation was a very simple one, which he had performed a number of times, and so on and on; but to no avail.

The next morning when he went in to see the patient before the operation, he found him in an altogether different mood—calm, unafraid, cheerful even. The operation turned out as Dr. Finney anticipated, and when the man was well on the way to recovery the doctor asked him what it was in their conversation that had relieved him of his fear. The man grinned and said, "Dr. Finney, nothing that you said helped me at all. I was awake most of the night, and trembled so in my fear that I wondered if the bed would not fall down. The colored orderly came in early, and asked, 'What's going to happen to you today, Boss?' I replied, 'I'm going to be operated on.' 'Who's your doctor?' 'Dr. Finney.' 'Pshaw, Dr. Finney's patients always gits well!' With that, my fear seemed to leave me and I felt like a new man." I am sure that the orderly had no particular standing in the medical profession of that city, and that he could not have been so attractive a person as Dr. Finney, yet what the famous doctor could not do through argument, the orderly did through a casual remark.

The power of suggestion is heightened when several are in *agreement* with what one says. A group that seems unanimous in its opinion about anything exerts strong pressure upon all of its members, especially on those who are younger and without prestige. A careful study of a number of colleges, taking this into consideration, reported that "the college fraternity is the most effective school of character education in the world."

Hitler made us aware that the power of suggestion is increased by *repetition*. When we hear a half-truth, or an evident untruth, over and over and over again, before too long we begin to wonder if after all it may not be fact.

Now, *let us superimpose these laws upon the home.* A child has little knowledge in any field, his experience is very limited, and certainly he hasn't organized what he knows into a system by which he can test what his parents may say.

His parents have acquired prestige. They are mother and father and have a standing that no others can possibly possess.

They have personal prestige. They are the great figures on his horizon. They know so much more than he does, they can do so many things that are beyond him. He begins to believe that their knowledge and their abilities are without limit. Of course, the time will come when there will be a rude awakening from this dream of his parents as near-gods; but that may not be for several years.

Much of the conversation in the home is indirectly suggestive. People talk in the child's presence and to him without appearing to try to influence his thinking, or his conduct.

The family group seems for the most part in agreement concerning the things about which its members talk. The united opinion of the group will be almost compulsive in its influence upon the younger boys and girls. Especially is this true if there are older brothers and sisters. Grandparents and other relatives often come into the home.

The conversation, too, is repetitious. At breakfast, dinner, and supper, day after day after day, the same ideas are expressed about things and about people; the same ideals, high or low, are held before the child's mind until he almost has to believe. Or, to put it differently, he believes without knowing how he has been led to believe, or why he believes as he does. The family traditions and convictions are passed on in this way from one generation to another.

It is not surprising that a number of graduate students at the University of Chicago, when asked where they got their major ideas in morals and religion, replied, "Through the conversation in our family at mealtime." Some of our more scholarly students of the family, like Dr. James Bossard of the University of Pennsylvania in *The Sociology of Child Development*, emphasize the influence of family conversation, especially at the table when its members are relaxed.

## II. The Principle of Sympathy

There is the tendency on our part to feel as those around us feel. We don't understand very well how it operates, but we are sure that it belongs to our life. One of our children, with her son under four months old, visited us several years ago. The baby was put to bed for his nap every morning at a certain hour. Day after day he slept soundly without fail. But the day came when they were to leave in the late afternoon. Earlier in the day there was a certain amount of excitement and strain incident to packing and the last-minute preparations for departure. There was, too, a feeling of regret on the part of all of us. When that morning the baby was laid down in the crib by his mother, with the confident expectation that he would go to sleep at once, nothing seemed farther from his mind. He began to toss and turn and cry, and was so unhappy that he had to be taken up and held. That morning he would not and did not take his nap. Something of the spirit of the household that day had been imparted to him, though he could understand no word that was spoken.

Let us look at this a little further. If the atmosphere of the home is one of love, because the parents love God, each other, their children, and their fellow men, then their children will respond to that love with answering love, and be prepared to love others with a love which, beginning in the family, broadens out as they come into touch with an increasing number of people, and reaches up to God. If the atmosphere created by the parents is one of trust, the children will trust as well as love. With love and trust pervading the home, peace will abide there, and serenity will dwell in the hearts of the children. More surely than in any other way will such an atmosphere deliver children from hate and suspicion, jealousy and fear.

Rose Alschuler, a leader in elementary school work, with this in mind said, "Know that it is better to live joyously with your children than conscientiously for them." While Rufus Jones, that gracious and wise Quaker, looking at the outcome in later life of the influence of contrasted homes, said that the first three years will determine "whether we shall laugh or cry, whether we shall make friends or travel a lonely path."[4]

## III. The Principle of Approval

There is the tendency on our part to believe and do what will win the approval of those whom we respect and to whom we are devoted. William James, who anticipated so much of what present-day psychologists are emphasizing, said years ago, "The deepest principle in human nature is the craving to be appreciated." We have only to look into our own hearts and to watch children to realize that this is pretty near the truth. Garry Myers has given us a pamphlet, which he calls *The Education of Young Children Through the Celebration of Their Successes.* In it he urges us to make memorable for the child the moment when he seizes the side of his crib and pulls himself erect for the first time. He would have us clap our hands, sing, dance, cry aloud, that the youngster might be encouraged to further endeavor toward growing up. We may not do just that, but all day long we are expressing approval or disapproval by tone of voice, gesture, smile, or frown. We say in effect, "This is right, do it; that is wrong, refrain from it." In this way we not only set up a child's goals, his ideas of right and wrong, but we thrust him in the direction of these ideals, because only as he follows them can he win our approval and escape our condemnation, which is a matter of great importance for him.

## IV. The Principle of Imitation

Still another tendency on our part is to do what we see people whom we admire and love do. There is *unconscious* imitation which is operative all the time. There is no endeavor on our part to teach, no effort on the part of the child to learn. We act in certain ways and, without either of us consciously purposing it, the child reproduces what we do. It is in this way that he learns our language. No one of us has put an infant in his chair and standing before him said, "Go to now, I am going to teach you how to speak English." We talk before him, and to him, and little by little he begins to talk as we do, sometimes to our distress, as he repeats our mistakes in grammar, our mispronunciations, our provincialisms, all of which probably we learned from our parents in the same way.

What is true of language is also true of manners and morals. A cartoon pictured a puzzled father, with his elbows on the dinner table, looking down its length at his wife and complaining, as he saw the children assuming his position, "Why can't they know that it is wrong for everybody but me to sit this way!" It was something like this that provoked a wag to say, "Children are born mimics; they behave like their parents, despite all our efforts to teach them manners."

We must not forget *conscious* imitation. Children deliberately try to do what those whom they esteem do. One day I stepped into the room of one of our sons and found him before the mirror diligently brushing his unruly hair. "What are you doing?" I asked. What foolish questions we put to our children! But this time I learned something that went deep. He replied, "I'm trying to be like you." Of course it made no difference how he parted his hair; on the right-hand side, or the left, or down the middle; or whether he slicked it back, or got a crew cut so he need not brush it at all. What concerned me was the possible deeper significance of his words. I was solemnized by the thought that he might really be trying to be like me in the more important aspects of life.

Every year some of our students carry questionnaires to boys and girls who live near the Seminary. Their answers make interesting reading. Let me quote a few questions and answers verbatim. "Whom would you rather be like?" "Mother." "Why?" "Because I like her ways." "Whom would you rather be like?" "Daddy." "Why?" "Because he is such a good sport." "Daddy." "Why?" "Because he just suits my notion of a man." I wish that had been my boy! "Daddy." "Why?" "Oh, you know, it is just natural for a boy to want to be like his daddy." And, let me add, for a girl to want to be like her mother.

But through the operation of these laws it is natural for a boy to be like his daddy, whether or not he puts his mind to it, and for a girl to be like her mother. I have separated these laws only for the purpose of discussion; they intermesh and work together with strong effect in the daily life of boys and girls with their parents in the home.

So much of the difficulty we experience when grown results from attitudes and habits of conduct which developed in our early years in the family through the unnoticed, yet almost inexorable, operation of these laws. Our early experiences go deep and abide. Why are we prejudiced toward the Negro, or the Jew, or toward members of certain classes, or certain kinds of work? Did our parents discuss with us the problems involved in race relations, indicating at length why it was wrong from the biological, sociological, and psychological standpoints for white and colored people to associate?

Did we not simply catch their attitudes, watch their conduct, listen to their use of words like "chink," "sheeny," which are loaded with the scorn of one who holds a superior position?

It is hard to change attitudes which have been created in this way. They did not enter life through argument, and it is almost impossible to evict them through reasoned statements. Even if we achieve a certain intellectual emancipation from some of our ideas acquired in childhood in the home, our emotions may be so seriously involved that we could hardly act upon the new truths to which our minds have given assent.

Dr. Goodwin Watson tells the striking story of a young Jew who came to this country from Russia. He was raised in Joppa in an orthodox family and became as a boy a Hebrew of the Hebrews. In his late teens he went to Russia, and was divested of the essential elements of his ancestral faith through his experience in a group of young Communists. Arriving in America he entered the University of Chicago. One day, with a friend, he sat down in a restaurant, leaving him to give the order. He liked what was served very much. A day or two later he returned to the restaurant and had the same waiter, who recognized him. "Bring me," he told him, "what I had before." He enjoyed it with equal relish. The next day he was back in the restaurant and asked the waiter for the same meal. As he was eating it with gusto, he thought, "I had better find out what this is so I can order it by name. I may not always find this waiter." When asked, the waiter said, "You have been eating spareribs." "What are spareribs?" "Pork, a part of the hog." When he heard that, he was almost actively sick, and had to leave the table and restaurant. Intellectually he had no shred of the faith of his fathers left. But the experiences of those early years in a pious family had affected his very viscera, and no reasoning on his part could make him inwardly comfortable while eating pork.[5]

If there were time, we might look at the prejudices which make it difficult to think clearly on many subjects, and difficult to change our attitudes and conduct, even when we know that our life is out of harmony with God's will.

## V. The Principle of Belief

There is one more principle at which we shall look. There is a tendency on our part to interpret the real belief of others on the basis of what they do, rather than what they say. This principle is tied in with the others we have been considering, but merits special examination. It is one with which we are familiar. It is embodied in an aphorism attributed to almost every great man from Demosthenes to Emerson, "What you do thunders so loudly, I cannot hear what you say."

The boy as he grows older, and this is equally true of the girl, begins to think, to put his ideas together, to work out some kind of a philosophy of life. He must interpret his family's faith by what he sees its members do. On that basis he must judge, for he cannot observe deeper motives, nor understand long-range purposes.

We *tell* our children so many things in the realm of religion, for we are concerned about their knowledge and faith; but on the basis of this law, what do we really *teach* them?

We tell them that prayer is the Christian's vital breath, but they never see us on our knees, nor hear our voices lifted in thanksgiving, or confession, or intercession. What do we teach them?

We tell them that the Bible is the bread of life; but they never catch us feeding our souls on its precious promises. What do we teach them?

We tell them that the Church is the pillar and ground of the truth, without which the Gospel would never have been preserved through the centuries, and could not be spread abroad today; but they see us attending its services irregularly, and giving to it grudgingly. What do we teach them?

We tell them that Sunday is the bulwark of our civilization, that if it goes, all goes; but they see us, under the spell of our highways and the lure of our fairways, making it a godless holiday. What do we teach them?

We tell them that God is our Father and that our future is secure in Him; but they see us taking anxious thought for the morrow. What do we teach them?

We tell them that Jesus is the resurrection and the life, and that in our Father's house are many mansions; but they see us sorrowing as those who have no hope. What do we teach them?

We tell them that Christ is not only our Saviour, but the Lord of life; yet they see us making our major decisions and engaging in our everyday duties irrespective of His will. What do we teach them?

Let me illustrate what I have been saying. A Y.M.C.A. secretary, knowing my interest in boys, called me into his office one day to show me a questionnaire a twelve-year-old boy had just handed in. The question was asked, "Do you have family prayers in your home?" The lad, writing with a pencil, had scribbled, "Yes." "When do you have family prayers?" He answered, "When company comes." I don't know what his parents told him about religion, but they taught him that the god of that home was public opinion.

A great Scottish preacher, John McNeill, who was captured for a while by the South Highland Presbyterian Church of Birmingham, Alabama, tells this story of his boyhood. One of the elders of his church verified it for me. His father worked in a quarry. Each morning he would get up at five o'clock, eat his frugal breakfast, fill his dinner pail, take his cap from its peg—all this without knowing that his son was often awake and watching him. Then he would open the door, and before putting on his cap, and leaving home, would bow his head and say, "In the name of the Lord I go forth to work." I don't know what that father told his son about religion; but he taught him that the God of that home was the God and Father of our Lord Jesus Christ.

We *tell* our children, also, a great many things about moral living, but again we must ask ourselves the question, what do we *teach* them?

We tell them about the joy and dignity of work, *all* work; but they see us go reluctantly to our tasks, or hear us speak in contempt of those who work with their hands. What do we teach them?

We tell them that purity is one of the qualities that separates man from the beasts; but they hear us telling an off-color story, or see us reading a salacious book, or going to a suggestive movie. What do we teach them?

We tell them that honesty is not just "the best policy" but that it is a fundamental virtue, a basic necessity in all human relations, without which a man, or a nation, cannot have any happy or confident association with his fellows. But they hear us understate their age as we go with them on a bus, or take them to a movie. What do we teach them?

We tell them that life offers not an opportunity for self-gratification, but a chance for self-discipline and service; yet they see us indulging ourselves as far as the law, or our finances, or public opinion will permit. What do we teach them?

We tell them that they should respect authority and obey the law; but they hear us constantly criticizing the law-making and law-enforcing bodies, and watch us dash through a red light or break the speed limit when we are sure no policeman is near. What do we teach them?

We tell them that we love them, and then turn them over to a nurse or a succession of baby sitters to raise. What do we teach them?

We tell them a thousand things day by day, for we earnestly want them to be better than we are; but of what value is our effort, if our speech is contradicted by our lives? Words and life must be in agreement if words are to be effective.

We make life harder for our children in another way. *Our lives are often inconsistent.* We not only deny our words by our lives; but the life of today may be contradicted by the life of tomorrow, so that their thinking is thrown into further confusion.

Let me illustrate this simply. Thanksgiving Day is approaching. We enter a home and find a very rich cake on the table and a two-year-old boy demanding a large piece. "No!" his mother says, "No!" Immediately he begins to cry, and as his crying rises to a scream, his mother surrenders. "All right," she says, "here it is, just a little piece, now run along and don't bother me." It is easy for him to work out his philosophy of life. His task is very simple. "If you cry hard enough you can get what you want." As he acts upon that he has his mother under his thumb.

In another home we find the same situation: boy, mother, cake. This boy, too, demands a generous slice. Again the mother says, "No!" Again scream follows scream; but there is a firm, "No! No!" which continued yelling does not change. For him, too, the process of developing a philosophy of life

is not hard. His conclusion is also simple, "Crying doesn't do any good," with the result that many a difficult situation is avoided in the future.

We enter a third home in the morning. Here we find the mother saying no and meaning it. But in the afternoon the boy returns to battle. Most boys will try a second time. "Cake!" he says, "Cake!" "No!" replies his mother, "No!" and we think the issue is settled. But just then she sees a neighbor, known for her gossiping tongue, coming up the walk. "C-a-k-e!" yells her son, "C-a-k-e!" We can almost see the mother's mind working. "What will this woman say about me if she comes in and finds me quarreling with my son? She will tell everybody that my home is a bedlam, and that I don't know how to raise my children." She is beaten. With that in mind she yields. "All right," she says to the boy, "shut up; here it is, take it and run along, and keep quiet." He runs off, clutching the cake; but his experiences that day have made thinking extremely difficult. He is bewildered. "This morning," he says to himself, "I cried, and I didn't get it. This afternoon, I cried and I got it. Now who can make heads or tails of this? How can I work out a sound philosophy of life which will guide me in all circumstances? I shall just have to stumble along on a trial and error basis."

Years ago Judge Ben Lindsey wrote a rather staggering book, *The Revolt of Modern Youth*. It would create no stir today. In it he said that yesterday we could chaperone our children. When a boy would do his ultimate for the girl of his fancy, he would hitch old Dobbin to the buggy, drive up to her house, and, while mother watched, she would trip lightly down the steps, be helped into the buggy, and they would drive off at the furious pace of eight miles an hour. You knew where they were then, and the community could keep its eyes

on them. But now, he says, all is different. A boy phones his girl from the drugstore, she walks down the street without telling anybody where she is going, his car glides up to the curb, she jumps in, and in an hour, according to the make of the car, the state of the roads, and his skill as a driver, they may be fifty or seventy-five miles away from home.

Without doubt, now we cannot chaperone them in the same way. But we can do a finer thing. We can build in them clear and strong ideals which will govern their lives wherever they are, whether our eyes are upon them or not. But we can be sure that we can't nurture such ideals in them when what we say today is contradicted by what we do tomorrow and when our conduct one day is negatived by the way in which we behave the next. Remember this, if you forget everything else, parents are teachers who have no holidays. We teach not when we wish to, but all the time, from the first waking sound in the morning until we tuck them in bed at night. We teach not so much by what we say, as by what we do and are. Family training cannot rise above family life.

The nation does rest on the cottage. The home is the cornerstone of education. The Church is dependent on the family. If the home fails, the State, and the school, and the Church cannot remedy that failure.

What our sons and daughters need as their problems multiply, what our nation needs as it faces these strange and terrifying days, and what the Church needs as it girds itself for a better witness, are parents who love each other and their children with an understanding and growing devotion; and who love God whom they have come to know in Jesus Christ, through whom alone true love is born and matures. It is the love of Christ, revealed in the Cross, that constrains us to love Him and others.

*ACKNOWLEDGMENTS*

# Acknowledgments

## Chapter 1

## Yesterday and Today

1. Ray E. Baber, *Marriage and the Family*, p. 93. McGraw-Hill Book Company, Inc., 1939.
2. Levy and Monroe, *The Happy Family* (Knopf, 1938). Quoted in Howard Becker and Reuben Hill, editors, *Family, Marriage and Parenthood*, p. 169. D. C. Heath and Company, 1955. By permission of Alfred A. Knopf, Inc.
3. Ernest Watson Burgess, "The Family in a Changing Society," in *American Journal of Sociology*, May, 1948.

## Chapter 2

## Love and Marriage

1. Source unknown.
2. Michel de Montaigne, "Friendship," in *The Selected Essays of Montaigne*, p. 149. (Adapted.) Carlton House, n.d.
3. Lewis M. Terman, *Psychological Factors in Marital Happiness*, p. 99. McGraw-Hill Book Company, Inc., 1938.
4. Josiah Royce, *The Philosophy of Loyalty*, p. VII. The Macmillan Company, 1920.
5. See Ephesians 5:21-31; Genesis 2:24; Matthew 19:5; Mark 10:7-8.
6. Count Hermann Keyserling, editor, *The Book of Marriage*. Copyright, 1920, by Harcourt, Brace and Company, Inc.
7. Royce, *op. cit.*, pp. 16-17, 121.
8. William and Mildred Morgan, *Thinking Together About Marriage and Family*, p. 56. Association Press, 1955. By permission.
9. Matthew 16:24-27.
10. I Samuel 16:7.
11. Isaiah 53:6.

12. I Peter 2:24.
13. John 3:16.
14. Philippians 2:3.
15. Psalm 15:4.
16. John 13:1.
17. John 15:13.
18. Henry Drummond, *The Changed Life*, p. 31. James Pott and Co., 1891.
19. II Corinthians 3:18. (Revised Standard Version.)
20. Adapted from Henry Drummond, *The Greatest Thing in the World*, p. 30. Dodge Publishing Co., n.d.
21. Henry A. Bowman, *Marriage for Moderns*, p. 327. Third Edition. Copyright, 1942, 1948, 1954, by the McGraw-Hill Book Company, Inc. By permission of the publisher.
22. From "To Love and to Cherish," in *The Reader's Digest*, October, 1939, p. 68. By permission.
23. *The Reader's Digest*, March, 1948, p. 37. By permission.
24. Robert C. Binkley and Frances Williams Binkley, *What Is Right With Marriage*, Chapter xi. D. Appleton and Company, 1929.
25. George William Brown and Ruth McAfee Brown, *Your First Week Together*. National Council of the Churches of Christ in the U.S.A., Chicago 3, Illinois.
26. Matthew 18:20.
27. Roy A. Burkhart, *From Friendship to Marriage*, p. 115. Harper & Brothers, 1937. By permission of the publisher.
28. John 15:15.
29. Acts 1:8. (R.S.V.)
30. Matthew 28:19-20.

## Chapter 3

## Love During the Critical Preschool Years

1. John Fiske, *The Meaning of Infancy*, p. 2. Houghton Mifflin Company, 1911. By permission of the publisher.
2. Arthur T. Jersild, *Child Psychology*, 4th Edition, pp. 33-34. Copyright, 1954, by Prentice-Hall, Inc., New York. Reprinted by permission of the publisher.
3. Reprinted with permission from Leonard Carmichael, editor, *Manual of Child Psychology* (John Wiley & Sons, Inc., 1946),

p. 299. (Quoted in Ilse Forest, *Child Development*, p. 52. McGraw-Hill Book Company, Inc., 1954.)

4. Ernest M. Ligon, *Their Future Is Now*, p. 102. Copyright, 1939. Reprinted by permission of The Macmillan Company.
5. Source unknown.
6. Quoted in Ruth Strang, *A Study of Young Children*, p. 64. Abingdon-Cokesbury Press, 1944. Reported by Katherine Reeves, of Cornell University, and used with her permission.
7. Helen Leland Witmer and Ruth Kotinsky, editors, *Personality in the Making: The Fact-Finding Report of the Mid-century White House Conference on Children and Youth*, p. 3. Harper & Brothers, 1952. By permission of the publisher.
8. Henry Clay Lindgren, *The Art of Human Relations*, p. 76. Hermitage House, Inc., 1954. By permission of Thomas Nelson & Sons.
9. Suggested by Fritz Künkel, in *What It Means to Grow Up*, Chapter I. Charles Scribner's Sons, 1936. By permission.
10. James H. S. Bossard and Eleanor S. Boll, *Parent and Child*, p. 298. University of Pennsylvania Press, 1953. By permission.
11. Arnold Gesell, *The Pre-School Child from the Standpoint of Public Hygiene and Education*, pp. 7-8. Houghton Mifflin Company, 1923. By permission of the publisher.

## Chapter 4

## Love During School Days

1. Rudyard Kipling, in "The Elephant's Child." From *Just So Stories*, by Rudyard Kipling. Copyright 1900 by Rudyard Kipling. Reprinted by permission of Mrs. George Bambridge and Doubleday & Company, Inc.
2. Christabel Morley Cordell, "Misbehavior Pattern," in the *Ladies' Home Journal*, May 1947. Copyright 1947 by The Curtis Publishing Company. Used by permission of author and publisher.
3. James H. S. Bossard, *The Sociology of Child Development*, pp. 79-80. Harper & Brothers, 1948. By permission of the publisher.

## CHAPTER 5
## Love and Adolescence

1. Esther Loring Richards, *Behaviour Aspects of Child Conduct*, p. 206. The Macmillan Company, 1934. By permission.
2. Goodwin Watson, *Youth After Conflict*, p. 48. Association Press, 1947. By permission.
3. Luella Cole, *Psychology of Adolescence*, p. 69. Rinehart and Company, Inc., 1954. By permission.
4. George H. Preston, *The Substance of Mental Health*, p. 119. Copyright, 1943. By permission of Rinehart & Company, Inc.
5. Robert J. Havighurst and Hilda Taba, *Adolescent Character and Personality*, pp. 71-72. John Wiley & Sons, Inc., 1949.
6. Adapted from Hamlin Garland, *A Son of the Middle Border*, pp. 177-178. The Macmillan Company, 1917.
7. I Corinthians 15:33. (R.S.V.)
8. John 10:10.
9. Marguerite Malm and Olis G. Jamison, *Adolescence*, pp. 415, 416, 417. McGraw-Hill Book Company, Inc., 1952. By permission of the publisher.
10. From an address by Harold T. Christiensen, Chairman of the Division of Education and Applied Psychology, Purdue University. In *The Torch*, July, 1952, p. 36.
11. F. A. Iremonger, *William Temple, Archbishop of Canterbury: His Life and Letters*, pp. 448-449. Oxford University Press, 1949. By permission of the publisher.
12. Richard C. Cabot, *Christianity and Sex*, pp. 7-8. Copyright, 1937. By permission of The Macmillan Company.
13. O. Spurgeon English and Gerald H. J. Pearson, *Emotional Problems of Living*, p. 76. W. W. Norton & Co., 1945. By permission.
14. Malm and Jamison, *op. cit.*, p. 406. By permission.
15. *Ibid.*, p. 417. By permission.

## CHAPTER 6
## Love Interacts

1. Nels F. S. Ferré, *Strengthening the Spiritual Life*, p. 39. Harper & Brothers, 1951. By permission of the publisher.

2. Horace Bushnell, *Christian Nurture,* pp. 211-212. Charles Scribner's Sons, 1888, 1916.
3. Frank Howard Richardson, *Parenthood and the Newer Psychology,* pp. xiii-xiv, 76-77. G. P. Putnam's Sons, 1926.
4. Rufus Jones, *Finding the Trail of Life,* pp. 17-18. Copyright, 1926, 1950. By permission of The Macmillan Company.
5. Goodwin Watson. Quoted from memory from a brochure put out some years ago by *The Inquiry,* 129 East 52nd St., New York.